T0365715

Cambridge Elements

Elements in Politics and Communication
edited by
Stuart Soroka
University of California

POLITICAL REPRESENTATION AS COMMUNICATIVE PRACTICE

Fabio Wolkenstein
University of Vienna

Christopher Wratil
University of Vienna

CAMBRIDGE
UNIVERSITY PRESS

Shaftesbury Road, Cambridge CB2 8EA, United Kingdom

One Liberty Plaza, 20th Floor, New York, NY 10006, USA

477 Williamstown Road, Port Melbourne, VIC 3207, Australia

314–321, 3rd Floor, Plot 3, Splendor Forum, Jasola District Centre,
New Delhi – 110025, India

103 Penang Road, #05–06/07, Visioncrest Commercial, Singapore 238467

Cambridge University Press is part of Cambridge University Press & Assessment,
a department of the University of Cambridge.

We share the University's mission to contribute to society through the pursuit of
education, learning and research at the highest international levels of excellence.

www.cambridge.org
Information on this title: www.cambridge.org/9781009565387

DOI: 10.1017/9781009416092

When citing this work, please include a reference to the DOI 10.1017/9781009416092

First published 2025

A catalogue record for this publication is available from the British Library

ISBN 978-1-009-56538-7 Hardback
ISBN 978-1-009-41610-8 Paperback
ISSN 2633-9897 (online)
ISSN 2633-9889 (print)

Additional resources for this publication at www.cambridge.org/wratil

Political Representation as Communicative Practice

Elements in Politics and Communication

DOI: 10.1017/9781009416092
First published online: March 2025

Fabio Wolkenstein
University of Vienna

Christopher Wratil
University of Vienna

Author for correspondence: Christopher Wratil,
christopher.wratil@univie.ac.at

Abstract: It is uncontroversial that the quality of democracy is closely bound up with the quality of political representation. But what exactly is political representation and how should we study it? This Element develops a novel conceptual framework for studying political representation that makes the insights of recent theoretical work on representation usable for quantitative empirical research. The theoretical literature the authors build on makes the case for changing the understanding of representation in two ways. First, it proposes to conceive representation in constructivist terms, as a practice that is shaped by both representatives and represented. Second, it treats communicative acts by representatives that address constituents and different analytical dimensions contained in them as the central categories of analysis; political representation is thus conceived as an essentially communicative practice. This Element argues that quantitative research can benefit from taking these innovations seriously, and it provides the conceptual tools for doing so.

Keywords: political representation, political communication, constructivism, democratic theory, quantitative methods

ISBNs: 9781009565387 (HB), 9781009416108 (PB), 9781009416092 (OC)
ISSNs: 2633-9897 (online), 2633-9889 (print)

Contents

1 Introduction

Political representation is at the core of modern democracy's legitimacy and functioning. It is the central practice through which citizens can exercise political influence and rule as a collective. But what is political representation at bottom? How can we define it? What different aspects of representation should we consider? And, how can we empirically study and normatively assess representation? These are the big questions we seek to revisit in this Element.

While political representation has been studied for decades, research on the topic has increasingly arrived at a dead end. Evidence from empirical studies continues to accumulate but it barely increases our understanding of representation. Our suggestion to overcome this impasse is to rethink the basic tenets on which empirical representation research is built: the implicit and explicit assumptions about representation made by researchers, the theoretical conceptions of representation they operate with as well as the norms and practices that guide empirical investigations. We will show that much quantitative-empirical work on representation relies on limiting assumptions about what representation is and takes an unduly narrow perspective on what aspects of representation are worth studying, thus risking to miss significant parts of the picture. In response, we outline an alternative approach that treats representation as a form of communication between representatives and citizens. It argues, in a nutshell, that in every communicative interaction between citizens and representatives, relevant information about different dimensions of representation is expressed. This is what scholars of representation should be interested in.

At the most abstract level, we define political *representation as a relationship between citizens and politicians that arises when citizens positively evaluate communicative acts that politicians perform in their capacity as holders of institutionalized political roles.* Defining representation in these terms opens up the concept to include phenomena often not considered to be part of representation and challenges common understandings of the term.

First, the idea of representation as a *relationship* highlights that both sides – citizens and politicians – contribute to representation: they *jointly* construct, create, and shape representation through personal or impersonal interactions (Disch, 2015; Montanaro, 2018; Saward, 2010, 2018). This contrasts with much research that treats the relationship between politicians and citizens as unidirectional, with the representative taking a passive "principal or constituency as its reference point" (Disch, 2015, p. 489). Instead of focusing only on politicians (as "agents" whose constituents are the "principal"), we should also pay attention to what citizens demand or desire in their interactions with politicians, how they view their relationship with them, and how they react to politicians' attempts to represent them.

Second, in a relational understanding of representation, elections and electoral connections between citizens and politicians (e.g., someone voting for a political candidate) are neither necessary nor sufficient for representation. Politicians may care about citizens who have never elected them (think of a national president who communicates their allegiance to *all* citizens, even those that have voted against them, or a member of parliament concerned with policies for asylum seekers or immigrants without citizenship, who have no right to vote). Similarly, politicians that run in unfree or staged elections, or come to power without elections at all, may still be representatives (albeit not properly *democratic* ones) if their communicative acts are positively evaluated by citizens (e.g., Truex, 2016). Conversely, the fact that someone voted for a specific politician does not *necessarily* constitute a representative relationship between this person and the politician. For instance, when citizens vote habitually for a particular party without any interest in, or expectations toward, its candidates or policies, no representative relationship is constituted.

Third, a relational understanding of representation suggests that a broad range of communicative acts performed by politicians are potentially of analytical interest for the study of representation. How politicians speak on television, present themselves on social media, vote in parliament, communicate their messages during election campaigns, etc. (as well as voters' evaluations of these acts) – all of this may be relevant for understanding the quality of representation. In this way, our approach differs markedly from the approach taken in the perhaps largest empirical literature on representation, which focuses on *policy responsiveness* (e.g., Gilens, 2012; Lax & Phillips, 2011; Soroka & Wlezien, 2010). Policy responsiveness scholarship typically adopts a "systemic" understanding of representation, studying whether elected politicians collectively deliver policy outputs in line with majority preferences. Representation thus understood is the result of a multitude of communicative acts that different political agents perform. However, this systemic way of conceiving representation diverts attention from a variety of communicative acts that are performed at the "dyadic" level between individual citizens or a group of citizens, and a single politician (e.g., "group appeals"). These are not the focus of policy responsiveness scholarship, but may be vital to the constitution and maintenance of representative relationships.

1.1 The Case for Studying Representation Differently

From our perspective, the most pertinent scientific aim of the study of representation should be to explain the state and changes of how citizens assess their relationship with politicians. Explaining citizens' assessment of their relationship with politicians is so important because citizens' approval of representation forms the basis for its (democratic) legitimacy (see, e.g., Saward, 2010; Saward, 2019). Hence, if we want to understand when and how representation becomes legitimate – for instance, to make it more legitimate in the future – we must first understand when citizens approve of representative relationships (also see Section 3.3). To see that we are currently not making much progress on this count, consider the stark contrast between political scientists' assessment of the state of representation and citizens' assessment of their relationship with politicians as holders of institutionalized political roles.

There is a vast scholarly literature arguing that a grave "*crisis of political representation*" – a worsening of the citizen–politician relationship over time – is haunting Western democracies today. One strand of the "crisis" literature has focused on political elites' tendency to manipulate citizens' political preferences instead of acting on them. In *Politicians Don't Pander: Political Manipulation and the Loss of Democratic Responsiveness*, Jacobs and Shapiro (2000) argue that increasing ideological polarization in Washington has made it harder for US presidents to substantively represent citizens' preferences in policy-making. Accordingly, they attempt to manipulate citizens' views through the use of crafted talk, slogans and symbols. The availability of opinion polls, focus groups, and other modern techniques to elicit and monitor citizens' preferences is primarily used to find the best "spin" to change citizens' preferences, rather than attempting to represent their views (Geer, 1996).

A second strand of this literature problematizes the declining relationship between citizens and political parties. In the US context, Fiorina and Abrams (2012) show that parties have ideologically polarized during the last decades, while a large part of the American public still identifies as moderates with centrist views. From the authors' perspective, representation has deteriorated as parties increasingly focus their electoral campaigns and policy-making activities on their core electorates rather than on swing voters whose views are closer to the average citizen. In a similar vein, yet taking a comparative view, Rosenbluth and Shapiro (2018) argue that many political parties around the world do not focus anymore on what is "best" for a majority of citizens. Instead, the proliferation of parties (i.e., the trend toward multi-party systems) and purportedly democratizing participatory initiatives (e.g., internal leadership elections or US-style primaries) during the last decades have caused parties to focus mainly on their own activists, who tend to hold more radical views than the general public.

To be sure, some comparative analyses of parties' evolving role can almost be read as an antithesis to such arguments, while *also* diagnosing an imminent crisis of representation. Analyzing European party systems, for example, Mair

(2013) argues that parties have completely lost touch with their traditional electorates and ideologically close civil society organizations that connected them to specific constituencies. Reacting to this, they have reinvented themselves as professionalized "cartels" that limit political competition and jointly seek to exercise control over state institutions and public funds. Consequently, their willingness and ability to represent the diverse policy preferences of citizens is all but completely lost; their policy platforms are becoming increasingly similar. Some suggest, moreover, that these tendencies are reinforced by Europeanization and globalization. Several studies show that the adaptation pressures of European Union (EU) constitutional law and EU legislation, as well as pressures from global markets and global governance institutions, constrain parties in their policy choices (e.g., Ward et al., 2015). This too has made it harder for them to offer citizens meaningful political alternatives. Representation suffers as a result.

Despite these prominent analyses, the problem is that, in empirical data of how citizens evaluate their relationship with politicians, the alleged crisis of representation is hardly visible. Consider Figure 1, which plots citizens' mean "trust in politicians" on a 0–10 scale (ranging from "Not trust at all" to "Complete trust") in several European democracies over time. The data is taken from the European Social Survey rounds 1 to 10.[1] Trust can here be seen as one indicator of the quality of citizens' relationship with their politicians. Compared to other indicators, trust may be stickier, as it is formed through socialization and by experience with politicians over extended periods (e.g., Easton, 2009). The figure clearly shows level differences in how citizens assess their relationship with politicians. Citizens in some of the post-communist democracies in Eastern Europe (e.g., Bulgaria, Croatia, Czech Republic, Poland) have the least trust in their politicians, while trust is highest in the Nordic countries (e.g., Denmark, Finland, Norway, Sweden). However, more interesting, and important for our argument, are trends over time. While some countries show clear upward trends over the last two decades (e.g., Czech Republic, Estonia, Norway, Switzerland), trust in politicians remained largely unchanged in others (e.g., Belgium, France, the Netherlands, the United Kingdom) and declined in a few (e.g., Cyprus, Spain). In total, trust in politicians in Europe seems to have developed very differently in different countries since the beginning of the new millennium, without following any clear general or political geographical pattern.

Figure 2 plots a different indicator of how citizens evaluate their relationship with politicians, specifically agreement (on a 5-point agree-disagree scale) to

[1] www.europeansocialsurvey.org/data/conditions_of_use.html.

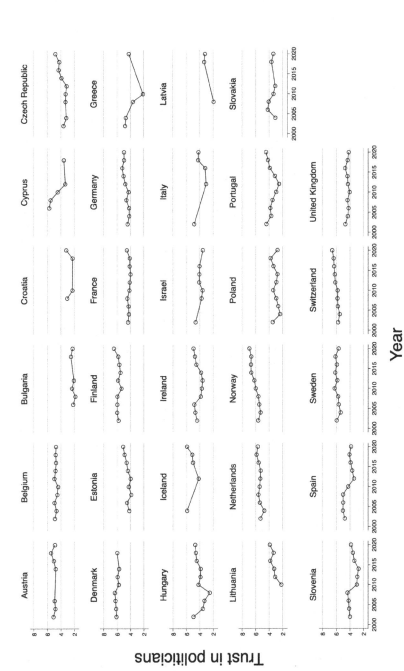

Figure 1 Trust in politicians from 2002 to 2020, European Social Survey (rounds 1–10)

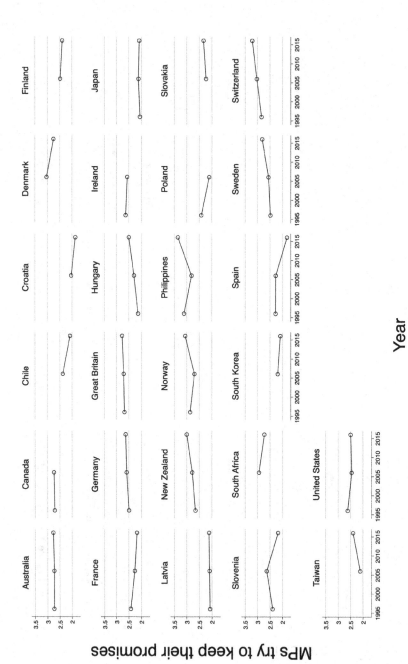

Figure 2 Perceived promissory representation from 1996 to 2016, International Social Survey Programme (1996, 2006, 2016)

the statement "[p]eople we elect as MPs try to keep the promises they have made during the election." Compared to trust in politicians, this is a much more specific indicator aiming at a performance assessment of a particular aspect of the citizen–politician relationship, that is, politicians making electoral promises to citizens and keeping them afterward. In Mansbridge's (2003) terminology, this is an assessment of the "promissory" component of representation. The data is taken from the International Social Survey Programme,[2] covering several Western democracies in up to three survey waves between 1996 and 2016, in which the question was included. Again, we cannot see any clear cross-country trend over time. Citizens' evaluation of politicians' efforts to keep the promises they made to them improved in several countries (e.g., Hungary, New Zealand, Sweden, Switzerland), but also declined in a few (e.g., Spain, Denmark).

From our perspective, these data are at odds with the notion that there is a deep-seated crisis of representation. In fact, both figures show level differences in how citizens evaluate their relationship with politicians across countries, with positive, stagnant as well as negative trends over time, and there is no evidence of a uniform downward trend in those evaluations. There is not even a significant group of countries that would have seen clear deteriorations of citizens' evaluations of politicians.[3] It thus seems that multiple highly influential analyses of the development of political representation in Western democracies are out of sync with how citizens evaluate their relationship with politicians.

1.2 Representation as Multidimensional Communicative Practice

How can we reconcile citizens' assessment of their relationship with politicians with the "grand stories" that political scientists tell us about representation? One possible explanation is, of course, that many existing analyses are simply wrong, and political representation is not actually in crisis. Along these lines, some scholars have suggested that the evidence for decreasing ideological congruence between citizens and the parties they vote for is actually very limited (Thomassen & van Ham, 2014). Yet, it would be rash to entirely dismiss the wealth of sophisticated analyses that document different kinds of crises of representation.

Instead, we propose that the crisis analyses may simply miss important parts of the picture of what representation is. These analyses share in common that they assume that the postulated crisis of representation primarily *manifests itself in the substantive dimension of the citizen–politician relationship.* Politicians

---

[2] https://search.gesis.org/research_data/ZA4747.

[3] In the Online Appendix, we also show that in time-series cross-section data on citizens' likability of parties and political leaders, there is no evidence of a clear time trend across countries – let alone any general decline in politicians' likability.

are thought to be increasingly unable or unwilling to advocate the policy views and preferences of citizens, and instead manipulate citizens' views, follow the preferences of narrow constituencies, exploit the state to secure power, or give in to international pressures. Yet, *other* aspects of the citizen–politician relationship than substantive representation might matter as well for how citizens evaluate elected representatives and representation in general. Our proposed way forward is to start by acknowledging this.

Notice that empirical representation scholarship *generally* tends to focus only on two aspects of the relationship between citizens and politicians, both of which can be traced to Hanna Pitkin's (1967) classic book *The Concept of Representation*. One is to what extent and under what conditions political actors adopt citizens' substantive policy views and advocate them in parliament, government, or the public sphere (e.g., Gilens, 2012; Lax & Phillips, 2011; Soroka & Wlezien, 2010). This is *substantive representation*, as mentioned a moment ago. A second aspect researchers commonly focus on is the degree to which politicians resemble their constituents with respect to various "descriptive" characteristics, such as gender, age, race, education, or social background (e.g., Dassonneville & McAllister, 2018; Sobolewska et al., 2018; Wängnerud, 2009). Following Pitkin, this is called *descriptive representation*. Only a small number of studies go beyond these two, arguably important dimensions of representation.[4]

What other aspects of representation might deserve our focus, over and above substantive and descriptive representation? Recent work in representation theory is a good starting point for answering this question (e.g., Mansbridge, 2003; Rehfeld, 2009; Saward, 2010). This body of work has uncovered additional dimensions of political representation, treating political representation as a multidimensional phenomenon with multiple facets that can be analyzed empirically (Wolkenstein & Wratil, 2021). It turns our attention to other aspects of the citizen–politician relationship that are currently largely outside of our field of vision, ranging from the justifications politicians offer for their decisions to the degree to which they try to present themselves in a more "personalized" fashion, as agents who act independently of their party and systemic constraints. What if politicians could "compensate" for the weakening substantive representation by, say, providing citizens with convincing justifications for their actions,

---

[4] In previous work, we have shown that various other dimensions of representation that have received significant attention in recent theoretical work on representation are largely absent in the quantitative-empirical literature (Wolkenstein & Wratil, 2021). In a random sample of 246 research articles on political representation that employed quantitative methods and were published in leading US and European political science journals between 2013 and 2019, 92 percent of all references to representation theory related to Pitkin's (1967) classic conceptions of representation.

personalizing their way of "doing politics" in forms that speak to citizens, and so forth? These sorts of questions must be investigated if political representation is to be properly understood today. Of course, this also means that we should not only study the behavior of politicians (or parties); we also need to invest our efforts and energies in understanding and explaining citizens' expectations and attitudes toward representation.

With this in mind, this Element aims to reset the study of representation by fundamentally questioning what aspects of representation we should examine and in what ways, with the ultimate aim of reconciling our analyses of representation with how citizens view representation. Some readers might think that we are attributing too much importance to citizens' judgments, especially in an age of "populism" and "democratic backsliding." Should we not reach for principled normative standards to evaluate the citizen–politician relationship, rather than focusing on how citizens perceive that relationship? While we think that other approaches certainly have their merits, we do believe, as Sabl (2015, p. 255) puts it, that "what ordinary people value is worth a provisional respect." And we should add that this is not an unfamiliar position. Many political scientists studying representation are ultimately – explicitly or implicitly – concerned about citizens' reactions to representation. This is why some ask questions such as: Does bad representation make citizens less satisfied with democracy (e.g., Dahlberg et al., 2014; Ezrow & Xezonakis, 2011; Mayne & Hakhverdian, 2016)? Does it make them question the legitimacy of the political system and its outputs (e.g., van Ham et al., 2017; Wratil & Wäckerle, 2023)? Does it make citizens more "populist" (e.g., Castanho Silva & Wratil, 2023; Halikiopoulou & Vasilopoulou, 2016)? In short, there is ample reason for giving citizens the leading word in the evaluation of representative relationships.

1.3 Structure of the Element

In the next section, we take a step back and revisit the most fundamental question: What *is* political representation? We outline four central categories that different models of representation are structured around: representatives, constituents, practices, and institutions. We then present three stylized ontologies of representation that are based on different assumptions about who can act as representative or constituent as well as which practices and institutions constitute and shape representation. We argue that an ontological position which we call "interactive constructivism" is the most plausible position. It allows us to conceptualize representation as a two-way relationship, in which citizens and politicians are both reacting to and influencing each other.

The possibility of reciprocal causation between representatives and constituents integrates a variety of views that different empiricists have on representation.

Building on this, Section 3 outlines our model of representation as communicative practice. At the center of our model are those communications between citizens and politicians that constitute representative relationships. We suggest analyzing these constitutive communicative acts by focusing on six theoretically derived dimensions of representation. We illustrate the argument with empirical examples of communications between citizens and politicians – ranging from tweets by former US president Joe Biden to statements by the German foreign minister Annalena Baerbock. Moreover, we argue that citizens' preferences regarding each dimension of representation are shaped by such factors as their partisanship, identity, or ideological predispositions.

In Section 4, we provide a case study of how representation can be studied using the relational understanding we favor, focusing on four rarely covered dimensions of our model. Specifically, we examine the representation of female voters by MPs during the 2019 general election campaign in the United Kingdom. Analyzing the speeches and voting behavior of MPs as well as women's preferences regarding different dimensions of representation, we show that female voters were better represented on some dimensions than others. In particular, female MPs did not emancipate themselves from their party leadership by regularly voting against the whip, although their female constituents desired them to do so. This illustrates how our approach can uncover deficiencies on dimensions of representation that are not commonly considered by most analysts today.

The conclusion summarizes the arguments advanced in this Element, and ends with a plea for greater theoretical sophistication in the study of political representation. Our proposed framework can hopefully provide a productive starting point for future research on representation – as a toolbox for researchers that can be used, revised, and expanded, rather than a one-size-fits-all theory that settles all relevant issues to do with representation.

2 Ontologies of Political Representation

Political representation can be conceptualized in various ways. Underlying different conceptions of representation are more fundamental ontological commitments, which are rarely made explicit yet have direct consequences for how we think about and study representation. In this section, we engage in theoretical groundwork and clarify what "ontologies of political representation" are currently available to us. We suggest that there exist three ontological options, which we call (1) *realism*, (2) *radical-democratic constructivism*, and

(3) *interactive constructivism*, respectively. We structure our discussion of the different ontologies by showing how they differ with respect to four central categories: (i) *representatives*, (ii) *constituents*, (iii) *practices*, and (iv) *institutions*. We end by arguing that *interactive constructivism* is the most appealing ontological choice. This sets the stage for the next section, which translates the theoretical insights of interactive constructivism into a framework for analysis that can be used by quantitative scholars.

2.1 Why Care about Ontology?

In political science and theory, the term "ontology" refers to assumptions we make about the nature of the social and political reality that is the focus of our analytical attention. But why should anyone interested in political representation care about ontology?

Argument 1: Ontology is antecedent to epistemology and methodology. The first argument for engaging with the ontology of representation is that ontological choices are logically prior to our epistemological and methodological choices; so, if we want to (a) understand what the major theoretical disputes in our discipline are fundamentally about, and (b) achieve consistency in how we study political representation ourselves, we must be aware of the ontological assumptions our analytical enterprises are premised upon. And, we must have a clear sense what these assumptions imply for our own as well as rival conceptual and empirical strategies.

To see this, consider first the link between ontology and epistemology. The assumptions one makes about the nature of the social and political reality to be investigated (ontology) have direct consequences for what one can acquire knowledge of (epistemology), and thus can study in a targeted and systematic fashion (methodology). With Hay (2006, p. 79), we might put the point more simply: "political ontology is intimately associated with adjudicating the categories to which legitimate appeal might be made in political analysis." Moreover, "even where we can agree upon common categories of actors, mechanisms, or processes to which legitimate appeal can be made, ontological choices affect substantively the content of our theories about such entities (and hence our expectations about how the political drama will unfold)."

Here is an example. If one assumes, as many scholars of representation do, that *constituencies* are entities that exist in some "objective" sense, say, in virtue of its members residing in a particular pre-defined electoral district (see Rehfeld, 2005, p. 35), then it makes good sense to try to acquire knowledge about the policy preferences of constituency members (and subsequently attempt to find out whether these preferences are shared by elected representatives). Using Hay's language, we may say that the category of "constituency preferences" can legitimately be appealed to as an independent object of analysis. In contrast, if one assumes that constituencies have no objective existence but are constructed by political actors who "*solicit* their objects" of representation by conjuring up images or symbols of what or whom is to be represented (Disch, 2019, p. 5), then any attempt to acquire knowledge about constituencies must start by looking at the speech acts or "discourses" through which political actors create constituencies. It might still be possible to appeal to the category of "constituency preferences," but that category cannot be studied independently of political actors' constituency-creating acts.

These different epistemological positions in turn call for different methodological choices. Scholars who believe that constituencies exist in some objective sense often use survey data about the policy preferences of, say, the residents of particular electoral districts or countries to, for instance, investigate the degree to which government policies or parties' political positions are "congruent" with those constituency preferences (see Sabl, 2015, pp. 346–348). Those who think of constituencies as the product of political actors' efforts to shape citizens' preferences, on the other hand, typically draw on various different methodologies, ranging from Essex school discourse analysis (e.g., Howarth et al., 2000, p. 45) to methods inspired by communication science that focus on how political actors' frame "representative claims" in the mass media (e.g., de Wilde, 2013), to survey experiments on "framing effects" (e.g., Druckman et al., 2013). What these diverse methods have in common is that they are geared toward studying political actors' attempts to create and mobilize constituencies, not citizens' supposedly "authentic" elite-independent preferences.

Argument 2: Key recent conceptual innovations come with alternative political ontologies. The second argument for studying ontology holds that anyone interested in political representation should care about ontology because important conceptual innovations in political theory have introduced alternative political ontologies into the field. We are referring, in particular, to the "constructivist turn" in representation theory, which constitutes the single most important theoretical advance in the last decades. Although some traditional approaches to conceptualizing political representation – such as the seminal work of Hanna Pitkin (1967) and Jane Mansbridge (2003) – also contain constructivist elements (see Disch, 2021, pp. 35–39), it was only through Saward's much-discussed notion of the "representative claim" (2010) and Disch's influential "mobilization conception of political representation" (2011, 2021) that constructivist approaches entered the political science mainstream. This is not to say that empirical scholars of representation have engaged much with constructivism; they have not (Wolkenstein & Wratil, 2021, pp. 863–864). But there can be little doubt that constructivism is increasingly widely accepted as an innovative and powerful theoretical paradigm, even in empiricist circles.

We have already touched on one key difference between constructivist ontologies of representation and what one might call more conventional "realist" ontologies: while realist ontologies treat the identity, interests and preferences of the represented as phenomena that exist independently of acts of representation, constructivist ontologies assume that "the identity, interests, or preferences of the represented are not given prior to representation but shaped through being represented" (Fossen, 2019, p. 824). This ontological shift has momentous consequences for how representation is conceptualized and empirically studied. For one thing, it redirects the focus of our analytical attentions to political actors' preference-, identity- and interest-shaping efforts. For another thing, constructivist ontologies decouple the practice of political representation from liberal democracy's representative institutions, notably parliament and parties, suggesting that nonelected actors, as well as politicians in authoritarian regimes, can (claim to) be representatives. This broadens our perspective of what political representation is about, and where it occurs, since claims to represent a particular constituency can in principle be advanced by anyone *within* and *without* democratic institutions (e.g., Saward, 2018).

Importantly, however, constructivism is not a unified paradigm that draws on a single set of ontological assumptions. It comes in different forms, and its proponents are not always explicit about the ontologies they operate with. In what follows, we distinguish two separate constructivist ontologies, which we call *radical-democratic constructivism* and *interactive constructivism*, respectively, and contrast these to the more familiar ontology of *realism* that many, perhaps most, empirical representation scholars (implicitly or explicitly) subscribe to. The presentation will be deliberately stylistic, bracketing numerous differences internal to the different theoretical traditions in order to highlight what is distinctive about them.

2.2 Four Central Categories of Political Representation

We will structure our discussion of the three different ontological options by showing how they differ with respect to four central categories: (i) *representatives*, (ii) *constituents*, (iii) *practices*, and (iv) *institutions*. We select these categories because it is difficult to see how any theory or conceptualization of representation could do without saying something about them. While we take these categories to be familiar enough not to require an extensive introduction, here is a brief summary of how we define them.

i. **Representatives** are agents who represent constituents, though the meaning of "represent" is subject to a degree of variation. Representatives can be individual agents or groups of individual agents (e.g., political parties). As Pettit (2010, p. 62) notes, moreover, in the case where a group acts as a representative, "the members may each act for their own ends, according to their own judgments, or they may act on a shared intention to further this or that end."

ii. **Constituents** are those who are represented by a representative. The category of constituents may also refer to single individuals or groups. As far as constituent groups are concerned, these may be defined by a variety of different characteristics: all adults with voting rights who reside within a particular electoral district may just as much count as a group of constituents as specific ethnic minorities (e.g., Mansbridge, 1999). Likewise, constituent groups may view themselves as groups, or merely be classed as groups by representatives (or researchers) without having a strong group identity of their own.

iii. **Practices** are, on our understanding, ideal-typical social actions related to political representation that may or may not be organized and enabled by institutions. With Max Weber (2013, pp. 3–62), we take "social actions" to be socially intended behaviors that, insofar as they are rule-oriented, imply institutions. Chief among the ideal-typical social actions that come to mind when thinking about political representation are *standing for others* (making others, who are not present, present by resembling them in some relevant sense), *speaking for others* (voicing concerns that others, who are not present, have or are assumed to have) or *acting for others* ("doing things" that are meant to be to the benefit of, or objectively benefit, others who are not present) (e.g., Pitkin, 1967). This list may, of course, be expanded.

iv. **Institutions** may, at the most general level, be described as embodied structures of differentiated roles (Miller, 2009, p. 25). Thus conceived, institutions consist of (a) formal and informal rules and norms that define particular institutional roles and (b) people who accept these roles. By giving the totality of defined roles a basic coherence, institutions ideally reduce uncertainty and coordinate individuals' actions in a way that allows them to act together, but some may also cause noncooperative, suboptimal outcomes (e.g., excessive veto points). Institutions that organize and enable political representation, such as elections and legislatures, assign particular roles to representatives and constituents (e.g., agents and principals), and provide spaces in which social actions that are related to political representation can be performed (e.g., giving a speech in parliament as *speaking for others*).

2.3 Ontology #1: Realism

What we call *realism* is perhaps the most well-known "ontology of political representation." It forms the basis of the most dominant approaches to studying representation in empirical political science. Let us unpack it step by step.

2.3.1 What Is Realism?

First, while those dominant approaches vary in terms of concepts, data, and measurement, they all converge on a similar understanding of political representation. Powell Jr. (2004, p. 273) summarizes this as follows: "representation means that the actions of . . . policy makers are supposed to be responsive to the wishes of the people" (classic accounts are Miller & Stokes, 1963; Soroka & Wlezien, 2010; Stimson et al., 1995). Of course, "simple correspondence between what citizens want and what policy makers do is not enough"; there must also exist "institutionalized arrangements that reliably create such connections. The most essential and irreplaceable of these institutions is the free and competitive national election in which all citizens can participate equally" (Powell Jr., 2004, pp. 273–274).

Second, in what sense is this way of thinking about political representation ontologically *realist*? It is realist because it assumes that the objects of analysis that are relevant to the study of political representation (e.g., the "free and competitive national election in which all citizens can participate equally") exist independently of our beliefs or the words and concepts that refer to them. Realism so conceived remains widespread among empirical political scientists, especially among scholars who apply quantitative methods. As Bevir (2008, p. 61) observes, this is a legacy of the intellectual climate of the mid-twentieth century, which was the era when the kind of political science that is still practiced today, and with it the systematic empirical study of political representation, first emerged (e.g., Miller & Stokes, 1963). The mid-twentieth century was generally a "hostile environment for metaphysics, and that environment could make it seem as if scientists might be able to decide ontological issues as they wished or even dismiss them as meaningless" because they cannot be verified or falsified (Bevir, 2008, p. 61). As a result, the rarely questioned view that social reality has a structure that is independent of our beliefs prevailed.

2.3.2 Core Categories

What do "realists" assume about the four core categories we distinguished? With respect to (i) *representatives*, this category is (mostly) assumed to be coextensive with "elected officials," that is, MPs who (usually) are members of political parties. Of course, depending on the electoral system of the polity under analysis, also groups of individual agents who act in a more or less cohesive way can count as representatives. In either case, it is conventionally assumed that representatives have interests, preferences, or, more generally, an agenda of their own, but also rational incentives to listen and act in accordance with what their constituents want (e.g., Mansbridge, 2003, p. 516). These incentives are supposed to be generated by the centrally important institution of elections, to which we turn in a moment.

This leads us to the second category, (ii) *constituents*. The standard assumption is that constituents are voters (i.e., people who possess the right to vote) within a particular geographical unit, depending on the constitutional design of the country under analysis and the research question(s) asked (e.g., an electoral district, a federal state, the entire polity). Alternatively, constituents could also be the members of certain sociodemographic groups, with their group membership being ascertained on the basis of "objective" characteristics (e.g., constituent A is treated as member of a particular social class in virtue of earning so-and-so much money per year). And, importantly, the preferences or interests of constituents are, at least theoretically (though not necessarily in empirical analysis, see Stimson et al., 1995), treated as simply given, i.e. exogenous. On one still-popular view, constituents' preferences are the product of rational calculations about their own "utility income," whereby each constituent compares "the stream of utility income from government activity he has received under the present government ... with those streams he believes he would have received if the various opposition parties had been in office" (Downs, 1957, p. 49). The possibility that the preferences of constituents are shaped by representatives is typically – and, again, in *theory* – hardly considered. (Some advocates of realism theoretically allow that representatives influence citizens' preferences through cues or persuasion. But they contend that the categories in which preferences are organized are pre-given and primarily relate to summative views about the desired policy mix that should be implemented, see, e.g., work on "policy mood" such as Stimson, 1999.)

With respect to (iii) *practices*, voting is the primary social action that is assumed to be relevant for constituents, for it is the act of voting that generates a representative relationship between representatives and constituents. Elected representatives, on the other hand, are thought to perform a variety of actions under the heading of "acting for" their constituents within legislatures and their parties: in parliament, they may vote for policies that they consider to be in the interest of the latter, and within their respective parties they may try to ensure that certain commitments are included in the party manifesto (see Pitkin, 1967, chap. 10). All of these practices are rule-oriented and thus imply (iv) *institutions*, and realist understandings of political representation largely limit themselves to theorizing formal institutions like elections, parties, and legislatures (e.g., Müller, 2003; Strøm et al., 2003). These institutions must be in place, realists would argue, in order for political representation to be possible in the first place. Above all, elections reliably create a connection between constituents and representatives, assigning to them the roles of principals and agents and providing a "sanctioning device" that induces representatives to act in a manner that is responsive to their constituents (Fearon, 1999, p. 56). The potential threat of being unelected by their constituents is believed to generate rational incentives for representatives to act for their constituents.

We want to stress that realist conceptions of representation come in a range of different forms that we cannot discuss in detail here (see, e.g., the sophisticated reconstruction of promissory and anticipatory representation in Mansbridge, 2003, pp. 516–520). What they all share in common is a strict focus on formal electoral representation as well as the underlying (though often tacit) ontological assumption that the institutions and practices that organize and enable electoral representation exist independently of our beliefs or the words and concepts that refer to them. On this view, political science, like the natural sciences, "reveals the world to us" (Bevir, 2008, p. 60) – a world in which constituents and representatives are thought to have a *real* existence. The next ontological option we consider offers a radical counter-image to this.

2.4 Ontology #2: Radical-democratic Constructivism

The term "radical democracy" is conventionally associated with a particular strand of post-Marxist theory that emerged in the 1970s and 1980s. The attribute "radical" typically refers to the intended radicalization of "liberal-democratic ideology." Liberal democracy is treated as a political form that allows for much deeper and wide-ranging social and political transformations than liberal democrats conventionally allow (Laclau & Mouffe, 1985, p. 176). Proponents of radical democracy defend this claim by arguing that our social and political reality is, at bottom, *constructed* by discourses and signs – an ontological claim that is diametrically opposed to realism. And since discourses and signs are malleable entities that can be dynamically shaped and reshaped by political actors, social conflict lines, political institutions, and so forth, can also be shaped and reshaped. Obviously, this ontological commitment has important implications for how we think of political representation. In this section, we want to examine *radical-democratic constructivism* by focusing on three influential radical democratic scholars: Claude Lefort, Ernesto Laclau, and Chantal Mouffe.

2.4.1 What Is Radical-democratic Constructivism?

The simplest summary of radical-democratic constructivism is that this strand of constructivism tends to see the entire social world as a product of representation. Lefort advances a *historical* argument in support of this proposition. His starting point is the observation that the emergence of modern democracy involved the "erection of a political stage on which competition can take place" – think, in particular, of parliaments (Lefort, 1988, p. 18). He then suggests that the continuous "staging" of political competition in democratic societies demonstrates to their citizens that "division is, in a general way, constitutive of the very unity of society" (Lefort, 1988, p. 18). By this is meant that the conflict-enabling arenas of modern democracies shape the *identity* of democratic societies by representing what a democratic society *is*, namely, an essentially conflictual enterprise where divisions may be procedurally tamed but not overcome. The divisions themselves are also the result of representations that political actors make by advancing diverging claims about who the people is, what society looks like, and so on. In doing so, political actors discursively bring these entities into existence.

In a similar vein, Laclau and Mouffe (1985) conceptualize representation as *articulation*, which denotes "any practice establishing a relation among elements such that their identity is modified as a result of the articulatory practice" (Laclau & Mouffe, 1985, p. 105). Articulation so understood is performative: it constitutes what is being articulated, for example a class subject or indeed "the people" as a whole. This view of representation is carefully distinguished from materialist, in particular Marxist, theories which assume that collective identities are a reflection of objective material interests (which would be a realist position). In particular, Laclau and Mouffe argue that the "unity" of collective subjects is never merely the expression of a common underlying essence but the result of political construction and struggle: "If the working class, as a hegemonic agent, manages to articulate around itself a number of democratic demands and struggles, this is due not to any a priori structural privilege, but to a political initiative on the part of the class" (Laclau & Mouffe, 1985, p. 65).

As we see in this quote, Laclau and Mouffe also reappropriate the originally Gramscian term of *hegemony* for their theoretical purposes. For them, hegemony and counter-hegemony refer to the "dis-articulation" and "re-articulation" of identities in an on-going political struggle, with the aim of discursively creating some "relative fixation of the social" (Laclau, 1990, p. 91). In Laclau's later work on "populism," many of these earlier ideas recur, though Laclau eventually shifts the main focus of attention to what he calls the *quintessentially political* task of constructing a "people." The act of constructing a people is, of course, not meant to occur ex nihilo; rather, it inevitably involves the re-articulation of already existing meanings, wherein "representation re-presents" (Thomassen, 2019, p. 336) those already existing meanings (see Laclau, 2005, p. 108). In fact, such re-articulations acquire much of their "force from citing representations of, for instance, the people that are already taken as authoritative" (Thomassen, 2019, p. 336). So, although Laclau rejects the idea that representation is about making interests or collective subjects that exist independently of representation "present" in the political sphere, he is not suggesting that any kind of collective subject or "people" could be constructed at any given moment and in any given context. Existing *representations* of what "the people" is always shape the horizon of articulatory possibilities.

2.4.2 Core Categories

Let us attempt to further clarify this first constructivist understanding of representation by looking at what radical-democratic constructivists have to say about our four core categories.

With respect to (i) *representatives*, Lefort has groups of individual agents in mind, notably parties that "offer competing interpretations of the present and of the future, thereby reminding us of the fact that our current situation is ambiguous and contains more than one possible future" (Geenens, 2019, p. 101). In Laclau and Mouffe's work, on the other hand, the focus tends to be more on single political leaders. Especially in his post-2000 work, Laclau is quite clear about the centrality of leadership to his "populist" theory of representation. It is indeed not difficult to interpret him as imagining representation as a *one-way relationship*, in which populist leaders "initiate a downward claim on a 'new' popular subject that displaces settled hierarchies and creates a new hegemonic order" (Jäger & Borriello, 2020, p. 743; see, e.g., Laclau, 2005, pp. 182–183, 99–100). Constructing a people, in other words, is not a process of mutual engagement between a leader and would-be constituents, let alone some sort of "deliberative" communicative process. Instead, it is a top-down identity-shaping exercise that instils in constituents a range of affective attitudes that Laclau (2005, pp. 53–56, 82–83) describes in terms of libidinal ties, a "love" for the leader and for all those whom the leader supposedly loves.

As far as (ii) *constituents* are concerned, Lefort seems to have in mind the generic category of citizens of a modern nation state, rather than more specific social groups. Lefort's citizens do not have any "objective" interests, however; nor do they constitute "substantial entities" as in realism (Lefort, 1988, p. 18). Both their broader self-identification as members of a particular society *and* their more specific partisan commitments and identities are shaped by the processes, conflicts, and so on that take place on the "political stage" (e.g., in parliament). For Laclau and Mouffe, on the other hand, constituents (Laclau speaks of "the people") are conceived as a collective subject that comes into being only through the construction of "a popular identity out of a plurality of democratic demands" (Laclau, 2005, p. 95). The individual demands or grievances are assumed to be somehow "out there" in society, though they are not a reflection of objective material interests, either. Representing these demands as linked together is, again, the task assigned to representatives (i.e., leaders), who, if successful, symbolically represent the unity of the collective. In Laclau's words, "the symbolic unification of [a] group around an individuality . . . is inherent to the formation of a 'people'" (Laclau, 2005, p. 100). Illustrating this point by using examples like Nelson Mandela and the Anti-Apartheid movement, Laclau suggests that the "name" of the leader can become synonymous with the collective of constituents that identify as a "people."

Moving now to (iii) *practices*, it seems to us that Lefort must assume that a broad variety of different (patterns of) social actions matter to representation. Deliberating in public, campaigning, debating policy in parliament, announcing court verdicts, and so forth – all of these things may be said to "construct and uphold the point of view from where citizens can see and understand themselves as members of this specific society," which is what Lefort considers the principal point of political representation (Geenens, 2019, p. 96). In Laclau and Mouffe's version of radical-democratic constructivism, arguably the primary practice that matters is articulation, that is (to again quote their instructive explanation), "any practice establishing a relation among elements such that their identity is modified as a result of the articulatory practice" (Laclau & Mouffe, 1985, p. 105). As we saw, this is what makes representation possible in the first place. Note that neither Hanna Pitkin's classic category of "acting for" constituents figures in radical-democratic constructivist understandings of political representation (Pitkin, 1967, chap. 10), nor does voting play any relevant role as a practice of representation.

Finally, with respect to (iv) *institutions*, the work of the three radical-democratic constructivist authors diverges most starkly. Lefort does not provide us with a comprehensive list of the political institutions of modern democracy that he deems central, but it is evident that he considers parties and parliaments crucially important vehicles for representing society. Indeed, he regards those institutions as "intimately interwoven with the very meaning of social life," since they allow citizens to make sense of society and their role in it (Geenens, 2019, p. 94). In this regard, Lefort has little in common with Laclau and Mouffe, whose work is famously characterized by a glaring "absence of considerations concerning the setup of the rules and procedures of political decision-making," or any other institutional considerations, for that matter (Westphal, 2019, p. 188). In fact, Laclau (2005, p. 154) even goes so far as to present the quintessentially *"political"* act of constructing a people as the opposite of the supposedly apolitical activities of traditional representative institutions, such as parties and parliament.

2.5 Ontology #3: Interactive Constructivism

The third and final ontological option we consider is also a constructivist approach, but one that differs in many respects from radical-democratic constructivism. First and foremost, what we call *interactive constructivism* does not regard political representation as constitutive of the entire social and political world but as *one* (nevertheless very important) set of political practices that can be studied within a wider array of practices. Second, interactive constructivism conceives representation in more procedural and relational terms than radical-democratic theories of "articulation" do; hence *interactive* constructivism. Well-known advocates of this view are Michael Saward, Nadia Urbinati, and Jane Mansbridge. These scholars certainly locate themselves within very different traditions of political thought, but they share a roughly similar understanding of what political representation is. And although they say rather little about ontology in their writings, they seem to rely on similar ontological assumptions.

2.5.1 What Is Interactive Constructivism?

Some representation theorists have taken note that there exist (at least) two different constructivist traditions. Urbinati (2019, p. 199), for example, explicitly distinguishes between a constructivism where the focus is on constructing a "people" (i.e., the radical-democratic type of constructivism of Laclau and Mouffe), and a constructivism that is concerned with the construction of "an *interpretative* or *artificially created similarity* between the representative and her electors" (Urbinati, 2011, p. 44). Constructing this sort of similarity requires, says Urbinati – and notice the difference between Urbinati's formulation and Laclau's talk of top-down articulation in particular – that representatives *cooperate* (Urbinati, 2019, p. 199) and *communicate* (Urbinati, 2011, p. 44) with those they wish to represent. Representation is here conceived as an interactive *two-way relationship*, not a one-way relationship created by a leader.

These ideas are presented in more systematic fashion in the work of Saward and Mansbridge, among others (2003, pp. 522–525, 2009, p. 370, 2018, p. 304). Saward's (2010) theory of representation as "claim-making" is the perhaps most well-known interactive constructivist account of representation, so we limit ourselves to presenting his account. In short, Saward frames representation in terms of a "claim" to be someone who stands for something that is presented by a claim-maker to an audience. As he puts it, "A *maker* of representation ('M') puts forward a *subject* ('S') which stands for an *object* ('O') that is related to a *referent* ('R') and is offered to an *audience* ('A')" (Saward, 2010, p. 36). Here is a helpful example that Saward provides to illustrate the idea (Saward, 2010, p. 37):

> The MP (maker) offers himself or herself (subject) as the embodiment of constituency interests (object) to that constituency (audience). The referent is the actual, flesh-and-blood people of the constituency. The object involves a selective portrayal of constituency interests.

Saward's account also has a strong *interactive* element built into it, in the form of audiences' capacity to question, contest, and reject representative claims. "Political makers of representations tend to want to foreclose or fix the meanings of themselves and their actions," argues Saward (2010, p. 54) – but "there is no representative claim that cannot be 'read back' or contested or disputed by its targets, recipients, or observers. The maker of a representative claim may intend that the constituents invoked by the claim see it as he or she wishes, but they are always to some extent free to reinterpret the claim, to turn it back against the maker: 'who are you to tell me who I am and what I need?'" Note that this is compatible with the notion that representative claims invariably are *constitutive* claims that construct "in some measure the groups that they purport to address (audience), along with the groups that they purport to speak for or about (constituency)" (Saward, 2010, p. 54). Those who are supposed to be constituted as addressees or constituents are not conceived as passive recipients of claims – as Laclau sometimes seems to present them in his version of radical-democratic constructivism (see Jäger & Borriello, 2020, p. 743) – but as capable of understanding that claims do not necessarily refer to natural or preexisting entities that exist prior to the claim being advanced. Hence, just as Urbinati writes, representatives need to cooperate and communicate with those they claim to represent if their claims are to be accepted.

With this basic understanding of interactive constructivism in place, we are now in a position to address the rather difficult second issue of which ontological assumptions this second constructivist view rests on. This is a difficult issue because, just like realists, advocates of interactive constructivism largely remain silent about ontology. Since interactive constructivists are mostly what may be called "mid-range" theorists, it makes good sense to begin searching for their ontological commitments at a lower level of abstraction. Consider Saward's (2010, p. 43) general proposition that "the world of political representation is a world of claim-making rather than the operation of formal institutions."

What Saward is saying is that particular kinds of speech acts – namely, "representative claims" – are the primary entities we can and should be interested in acquiring knowledge of when studying representation. Meanwhile, he refrains from making more ambitious statements about what the social or political world is. Indeed, Saward makes clear that "there are more things in the political world than claims – there are demands, for example. And not all claims are representative claims, though many will be, even if not explicitly" (Saward, 2010, p. 43). These propositions appear to be accepted by most interactive constructivists, even if they do not use Saward's language of "claims" or, like Mansbridge, deal with already-established representative relationships.

Arguably, a view of politics that assigns central importance to *communication* must be presupposed here. After all, it is various sorts of *speech acts* – claims, demands, interventions aimed at contesting claims, and so on – that are treated as the central elements of the political world. This also explains why leading interactive constructivists affirm the fundamental compatibility of their approach with deliberative democratic theory (Saward, 2010, pp. 3, 21, 31, 93, 108–109, 164–165), or even avowedly start from deliberative-democratic premises, as Mansbridge does. The question then arises whether deliberative democratic theory can furnish an ontological grounding for interactive constructivism? The difficulty with this is that deliberative theory, even in its most sophisticated Habermasian variant, is not explicitly concerned with ontology, either. That said, it is possible to read Habermas as committing to particular assumptions about the nature of the social and political world we inhabit, thus offering some relevant reflections about ontology that we can use for our present purposes.

One important ontological commitment in Habermas' work concerns the notion of popular sovereignty, which he reconceptualizes in strictly communicative terms. This involves a substantial revision of the social ontology underlying popular sovereignty: rather than thinking of the popular sovereign as an embodied collective, Habermas describes popular sovereignty as generated out of "subjectless" forms of communication that circulate in the public sphere in a way that is potentially detached from individual speakers. In his own words, "popular sovereignty no longer concentrates in a collectivity, or in the physically tangible presence of the united citizens or their assembled representatives, but only takes effect in the circulation of reasonably structured deliberations and decisions" (Habermas, 1998, p. 136; also see Habermas, 2006). He explains this idea by reference to Hannah Arendt's notion of "communicative power," a power that cannot be "possessed" by anyone but arises when people come together to jointly form opinions and wills (Habermas, 1998, pp. 147–151). The shared beliefs that are generated or reinforced in these processes of opinion- and will-formation can in turn animate people to act in ways that influence legislative and administrative institutions (e.g., when "convinced minorities," having formed shared beliefs, "dispute the legitimacy of existing laws and engage in civil disobedience," Habermas, 1998, p. 148). If we further accept that collective opinion and will formation constantly takes place in myriad different sites across society, then it is easy to see why Habermas views popular sovereignty as depersonalized and decentralized: democratic laws are typically influenced by innumerable, largely unpredictable processes of opinion and will formation, not by a single sovereign subject that asserts a coherent will.

Habermas' communicative reinterpretation of popular sovereignty strongly resonates with interactive constructivism. When would-be representatives make "representative claims," for example, they will often do so on the basis of prior processes of opinion and will formation (e.g., an MP advances a representative claim after discussing with other party members and aides how that claim can target the right audience). And when their audience communicatively reacts to a representative claim (saying, e.g., "Who are you to tell me who I am and what I need?"), their reaction may equally feed off earlier episodes of communicative opinion and will formation (e.g., they may have discussed with members of their football club what kind of politician they prefer). Note that there is also the possibility that claim-makers and audiences *jointly* engage in processes of opinion and will formation. The first thing that might come to mind here are old-fashioned New England town meetings, but there are many other sites where such discursive interactions might take place (see Neblo et al., 2018). At any rate, the point to note is that all of these instances of people making use of "commu- nicative power" may in more or less direct ways influence how political power is exercised, just as Habermas' revised notion of popular sovereignty suggests.

Habermas' suggestion to conceive popular sovereignty as residing in "subjectless" communication that circulates throughout society is closely linked to another ontological commitment. For Habermas (1998, pp. 302, 358), the exercise of "communicative power" "is internally connected with contexts of a rationalized lifeworld that meets it halfway," meaning that it must be "anchored in the voluntary associations of civil society and embedded in liberal patterns of political culture and socialization." Habermas' point is that processes of opinion and will formation require a historically grown background culture of taken-for-granted settings in which citizens can experience what Habermas calls "understanding-oriented communication" on an everyday basis. They must experience that they share interpretations of certain matters of concern with others, and that it is possible to arrive at shared interpretations through conversation (think, for instance, of a disagreement over dinner with one's family or neighbors about the interpretation of some current event). Only if such experiences are regularly made will citizens expect communicative interactions with strangers to bear fruit and be worth the effort, say, in terms of leading to joint action. This is crucial if they are to effectively engage with representative claims (or formulate counter-claims).

2.5.2 Core Categories

It is time to put all those pieces together and look at what interactive construct-ivism assumes about our four core categories. With respect to (i) *representatives*, it seems that any individual agent, or groups of individual agents that more or less speaks with one voice, can in principle be a representative if it advances what Saward calls a "claim" to represent others. The range of possible representative agents is in principle unlimited, and so are the reasons why they might claim to represent others (see Saward, 2018). The same goes for (ii) *constituents*, understood, again with Saward, as the group that representatives "purport to speak for or about" (Saward, 2010, p. 54). This simply follows logically from what we just learned about representatives. If representative claims are necessarily constitutive claims that construct "in some measure the groups ... that [makers of representative claims] purport to speak for or about (constituency)" (Saward, 2010, p. 54), and if anyone can act as a maker of representative claims, then there exist as many possible constituencies as there are possible representative claims.

As we have already mentioned, the central (iii) *practices* in interactive constructivist theories of representation are communicative practices (i.e., speaking for others), most notably the making of representative claims by would-be representatives, and the intended constituents' verbal reactions to those claims (e.g., affirming, questioning, contesting claims) in which their "communicative power" makes itself visible. These discursive interactions can take place in the media (e.g., when members of a particular group, say some ethnic minority, speak out in a newspaper about certain activists' or politicians' claims to act in those groups' interests). Sometimes they also take the shape of personal "two-way communication" (Mansbridge, 2009, p. 370) between rep-resentatives and constituents, for example in town hall meetings, campaign rallies, and so on (see Mansbridge, 2018). Of course, reactions to representative claims can also be nonverbal: for instance, if the constituency that a particular MP claims to speak for unelects that MP, this may be interpreted as a rejection of the MP's representative claim(s). These forms of nonverbal action are also, in a sense, communicative, for they can provide citizens with an effective way of expressing reactions to representative claims.

What role do (iv) *institutions* play in theories of interactive constructivism? This question may be answered in different ways. For Saward (2010, p. 44), it is clear that "[r]epresentation is a process of claim-making rather than a fact established by institutional election or selection; or at least, it can only be the latter by virtue of being the former." This does not mean that Saward considers institutions irrelevant (see Saward, 2018). The point is rather that institutions such as elections are not generative of representative relationships, as conventional realist ontologies of representation assume. Instead, representation *begins* with a representative claim. Other interactive constructivists stress that the making and uptake of representative claims inevitably takes place within a rich and complex institutional ecology that affects how those claims are framed and received, and what responses they are met with (cf. Habermas, 2006). Urbinati (2019, p. 201), for example, argues that "norms, procedures and institutions are always the horizon in which claims are made and recognized as representative." We will build on these considerations in our own theorizing.

2.6 The Case for Interactive Constructivism

In this section, we have presented three different "ontologies of political representation" (for an overview, see Table 1). The presentation has been stylized, but it has brought out what is distinctive about each ontological option. We end by arguing that the third ontology we discussed, *interactive constructivism*, is on-balance the best choice for an expanded and improved empirical research agenda on political representation that takes theoretical innovations seriously.

Recall, first, that *realism* assumes that constituencies and their preferences exist in some "objective," fixed sense, and that representatives primarily express these pre-defined preferences. This is an exceedingly restrictive view of representation. It is rather insensitive to the fact that the political identities, preferences and (perceived) interests of constituents can also be, and often are, shaped by representatives (a key takeaway of innumerable high-profile empirical studies on "framing effects" and "elite influence," see, e.g., Bisgaard & Slothuus, 2018; Druckman et al., 2013, also see Disch, 2021, that empiricists acknowledge but often do not fully incorporate in their theoretical frameworks). While realism, in its pure form, propagates a clear causal model, in which constituents induce representatives to act in a particular way by threatening to unelect them, interactive constructivism is based on the possibility of reciprocal causation, with both sides potentially influencing each other. In fact, it is maximally open to different causal models by simply acknowledging the co-creation of representation without positing any specific causal pathways. Realism is also unduly restrictive in that it overlooks that representative relationships are not always or necessarily generated (or terminated) by elections: even within systems of electoral representation, constituents may feel represented by

Table 1 Ontologies of political representation

	Realism	Radical-democratic constructivism	Interactive constructivism
MAIN ONTOLOGICAL ASSUMPTIONS	Political representation exists independently of our beliefs or the words and concepts that refer to them; representative relationships are generated and maintained by real-existing formal institutions	The entire social world is a product of representation; representation is generated through "discourses" within (Lefort) or without (Laclau & Mouffe) established democratic institutions	Political representation is a relationship that is constructed through communicative acts (e.g., claim-making and uptake); the underlying processes of opinion and will formation require a "lifeworld" that allows for meaningful communication
REPRESENTATIVES	Elected officials	Parties (Lefort); political leaders (Laclau & Mouffe)	Claim-makers
CONSTITUENTS	Voters (i.e., people who possess the right to vote within a specified geographical unit), members of particular social groups	Citizens of modern nation-states (Lefort); an "articulated" collective subject (Laclau & Mouffe)	Groups described by claimants, "audiences" (Saward)

Table 1 (cont.)

	Realism	Radical-democratic constructivism	Interactive constructivism
PRACTICES	Voting (constituents), "acting for" (representatives)	Deliberating in public, campaigning, debating policy in parliament, etc. (Lefort); "articulation" (Laclau & Mouffe)	Claim-making and reactions to claims
INSTITUTIONS	Elections, parties and legislatures	Parties and parliaments (Lefort); institutions as potential impediment to representation (Laclau & Mouffe)	Institutions are not *necessary* to generate or legitimize representative relationships, but provide the horizon in which representative claims are made and receive uptake

someone that they did or could not directly vote for – say – a representative from another electoral district (see Mansbridge, 2003, pp. 522–525). In contrast to this, interactive constructivism assumes that representative relationships are communicatively constructed by both representative and constituents, and it acknowledges the important fact that those relationships can also be nonelectoral.

Second, remember that the *radical-democratic constructivism* of Laclau and Mouffe is primarily concerned with the articulation of collective subjects, and has a strong leader focus and anti-institutional bias. This, too, seems needlessly restrictive to us. Especially the later Laclau's all but complete rejection of traditional representative institutions (e.g., parliaments) as meaningful sites of political representation disregards the complex relationship between constructivist representative practices and institutions that Urbinati (2019) rightly draws attention to. Interactive constructivism, while admitting noninstitutionalized forms of representation, has the virtue of not rejecting the possibility that political representation often may occur within formally institutionalized arenas. Nor does it deny that representatives' claims to speak for others are often shaped by numerous formal and informal institutions that affect how those claims are received by intended audiences, and how audiences can respond to them. What about Lefortian *radical-democratic constructivism*? This might be somewhat compatible with interactive constructivism, but to the extent that Lefort thinks of representation as a purely systemic affair that has "relatively little to do with the actual decision-making" within representative bodies (Geenens, 2019, p. 92), it would also seem to unnecessarily restrict its purview in ways that interactive constructivism does not.

One way of putting our point is to say that interactive constructivism is the *least restrictive* ontology of representation. This not only makes it the most attractive ontology, for the reasons we have just mentioned. As we will show next, interactive constructivism's nonrestrictive character also opens the door to conceptualizing and operationalizing political representation in a variety of different ways, as well as treating the conceptual and empirical tools that we develop in the remainder of this Element as a flexible and expandable, rather than institutionally or contextually limited, toolkit.

3 Political Representation as Communicative Practice

3.1 A Methodological Preface

Since the primary aim of our Element is to offer a novel mid-range vocabulary for studying political representation with quantitative methods, some limitations will apply to our theory building that create tensions with our broader ontological commitment to interactive constructivism. In our view, however, some tensions and trade-offs are acceptable so long as the resulting theoretical framework is coherent and can help advance the field, which we believe it is and can.

Resisting "expansionism." The first limitation that applies to our own theory-building is that we will have to resist the tendency of interactive constructivist scholars to expand the possibilities of representation and the signification of the term as widely as possible. While most interactive constructivist scholars contend that political representation should be studied beyond conventional institutionalized arenas (e.g., parliaments), and with an eye to innumerable nontraditional representative agents (e.g., unelected activists), quantitative representation scholars – our primary audience – will struggle to meet this latter requirement using the tools and resources available to them (in the following, we are reciting Wolkenstein & Wratil, 2021, p. 865).

First, in quantitative representation research, the primary dependent and independent variables that are currently studied – representatives' behavior and citizens' (policy) preferences – are usually conceived as *latent concepts*. That is, they cannot be observed directly but must be unfolded or scaled from manifest variables. This means that empiricists can study only a limited number of representative relationships, due to the costs of data collection for each indicator. These data demands are multiplied when assessing a variety of different kinds of preferences and behaviors, or when studying representation over time. And they are bound to become unmanageable when one attempts to study the innumerable representative relationships between citizens and local, national and international nonelected representatives (representation by activists, representation by globally known celebrities, etc.).

Second, using quantitative methods to study nonelected forms of representation faces serious challenges as far as sampling is concerned. Think, for example, of celebrities that claim to "give a voice" to (ostensibly) voiceless others: Saward's stock example is Bono, the U2 front man and philanthropist, who repeatedly claimed to "represent a lot of people [in Africa] who have no voice at all" (quoted in Saward, 2009, p. 1). The difficulties with sampling already become clear when we ask the basic question of what is the larger population of which Bono is an instance of and from which we could try to obtain a representative sample? If the population is "celebrities involved in politics," how would we get a list of all these celebrities? Perhaps even more challengingly: who exactly are Bono's constituents? All inhabitants of the continent of Africa? The fans on his Facebook or U2's Instagram page? These sorts of problems arise to a much smaller degree in the case of formal, electoral representation. Because of its level of institutionalization (e.g., lists of candidates, members of parliament, resident registration), electoral representation offers rather well-defined sampling frames.

For these two reasons, we will in what follows limit our focus to traditional, institutionalized forms of representation, that is, representation in the context of elections, parties, and parliaments. Although we will move beyond exclusively *electoral* representation, our frame of reference will remain domestic representative democracy, and the main representatives we shall focus on will be elected politicians performing institutionalized roles.

Can one be a constructivist and do quantitative research? The second and related limitation has to do with more fundamental tensions between constructivism and the presuppositions that much of quantitative social science rests upon. Quantitative scholars conventionally assume that, or unwittingly proceed *as if*, they are studying relatively "fixed objects of inquiry that possess observable and, at least to some extent, measurable properties, such that they are amenable to explanations in terms of general laws, even if these general laws sometimes involve assigning probabilities to various outcomes" (Bevir & Kedar, 2008, p. 504). Constructivists, in contrast, characteristically focus on the contextual, *understanding*-oriented study of contingent human meanings, and they tend to refrain from appealing to general laws of *explaining* human behavior (on understanding vs. explaining, see, canonically, Weber, 1978, pp. 4–26). Does that mean that one cannot be a constructivist and use quantitative methods without contradicting oneself?

If the answer to this were positive, arguably our entire project of formulating a novel constructivist theoretical framework for studying political representation with quantitative methods would be inconsistent. We would argue, however, following Bevir and Blakely (2015), that, contrary to widespread belief, the real clash is at the level of *philosophy*, not *methods*. What matters is not so much whether one uses qualitative or quantitative methods or quantitative methods, but, again, whether one commits to a constructivist or a realist ontology. One can be a philosophical constructivist (this is how we would describe ourselves) and use quantitative methods without risking self-contradiction, so long as one: (a) does not claim to be studying an observer-independent world, (b) remains sensitive to context and people's own beliefs and meanings, and, indeed, (c) is aware of the fact that, through studying representation in particular ways, one might engage in acts of "construction" oneself (e.g., when trying to elicit specific political preferences from citizens by asking certain survey questions, one might "construct" those preferences by giving a particular shape to them).

3.2 Core Components of Representation I: Representatives' Communicative Acts

We can now proceed by identifying two core components of political representation that will form the backbone of our novel theoretical approach:

1) *Representatives' communicative acts*, and
2) *Citizens' evaluations of representatives' communicative acts.*

In this section, we conceptualize *representatives' communicative acts*, that is, actions would-be representatives or representatives perform to communicate to citizens that they seek to act, or have acted, on their behalf. *Citizens' evaluations of representatives' communicative acts* will be the topic of the next section.

Let us begin by recalling how we have provisionally defined political representation in the introduction to this Element: *Political representation* is a relationship between citizens and politicians that arises when citizens positively evaluate communicative acts that politicians perform in their capacity as holders of certain institutionalized roles.

At the heart of this deliberately broad and general definition is the idea that political representation starts with a *communicative act*: a (would-be) representative with institutionalized political roles (e.g., a candidate running for office or an already-elected politician) "does something" that communicates to (would-be) constituents that the (would-be) representative seeks to speak and act for them. Political representation, in this sense, is a performative product: it is the performance of one or a string of more or less interconnected communicative acts that contribute to establishing or maintaining a particular state of affairs, that is, a representative relationship between citizens and politicians. The communicative acts in question will often be *speech acts*, but they need not be. There exist a variety of communicative acts that do not involve speech, yet communicate to citizens that the (would be) representative in question intends to speak and act on their behalf as a holder of certain institutionalized roles. We discuss these two species of communicative acts in turn.

Speech acts. The term "speech act" is most prominently associated with a strand of twentieth-century philosophy called *speech act theory*, which is concerned with the specific acts that the sentences we utter to one another are meant to perform: requests, apologies, predictions, promises, and so forth. Key speech act theorists include John Searle (1969) and J.L. Austin (1975), and interactive constructivists (and, incidentally, also earlier theorists of representation like Pitkin [1967, pp. 254–255]) often explicitly acknowledge their indebtedness to the works of these scholars. For example, Saward (2018, p. 278) clearly states, affirmatively citing Austin (1975), that political representation is something that is "performed ... in the speech-act sense." Indeed, for Saward (2014, p. 725), "Political actors do not simply occupy or exemplify (for example) types or forms [of representative agents] which exist independently of their actions; types do not have a practical existence outside their enactment as roles by agents. Inherent to the [speech] act of claiming – implicitly or explicitly – to represent a constituency is a constituting or reinforcing of the social availability of that role [. . .]."

The key takeaway is that (would-be) representatives constitute and play their "role" in two ways. (1) They *utter certain sentences* (e.g., in a public speech, on social media, in a TV interview, and so forth) *that are meant to perform the function of conjuring up a particular image of themselves.* For instance, a representative might state that they have grown up as members of a particular social class or minority, thus conjuring up the image of being capable to empathize with and understand the concerns of those who belong to that class or minority. (2) Representatives might also *perform actions that do not involve speech but are meant to reinforce, or resonate with, the image that the (would-be) representative would like to conjure up.* An example would be to appear at a public protest to communicate solidarity with a specific social class or minority.

Figure 3 Example of a speech act

Note: Official portrait of Joe Biden retrieved from www.whitehouse.gov, used under CC BY 3.0/Text box has been added by the authors.

Before we get to these latter types of communicative acts that do not involve speech, we unpack communicative speech acts.

Regarding communicative acts involving speech, what is meant by *sentences through which (would-be) representatives seek to conjure up a particular image of themselves* (1), and how do these sentences *perform* something in the speech-act sense? Figure 3 depicts a public statement made by then-presidential candidate Joe Biden in early October 2020, in which he declares that he will represent American citizens irrespective of whether or not they voted for him should he get elected into the White House. Most obviously, this utterance performs a *promise* ("I will be an American president"). It also performs the function of presenting the wider public the broader self-image that Biden sought to cultivate throughout his campaign, namely the image of a "conciliatory" candidate, the "elder statesman" who strives to unite the deeply polarized country and aims at the good of the whole nation. Using Saward's language, we may say that Biden's utterance (and many connected utterances, for example, "[l]et this grim era of demonization in America begin to end – here and now")[5] are part of him *enacting* a particular representative role that does not exist independently of him enacting it. That is to say, Biden is not in some "objective" sense a (would-be) political representative who embodies the type of the "elder states-man" who seeks to overcome divisions and rule in the name of the common good; he *constitutes* this persona through (repeatedly) saying things (and performing acts that do not involve speech) that are meant to signal to citizens that this is who he is.

Speech act theory figures in different ways in different versions of interactive constructivism. In Mansbridge's work, it enters through the backdoor of the particular, Habermasian brand of deliberative democratic theory she endorses. Mansbridge stresses in many of her articles the importance of meaningful deliberative encounters between representatives and constituents (Mansbridge, 1999, pp. 641–643, 2003, p. 525, 2009, pp. 384–386; Mansbridge, 2018, pp. 305–307). She argues that "good democratic representation must rest in part on the capacity of representatives to hear, to respond, to explain legislative actions, and to act on citizens' responses to those explanations" (Mansbridge, 2018, p. 307). The theoretical underpinning to this argument, famously laid out by Habermas (1981, esp. pp. 385–427), draws, among other things, on the speech act theories of Austin and Searle, and suggests that the level of what is *performed* through speech acts (e.g., a promise – "I will be an American president") is the level at which mutual understanding must occur in deliberative

---

5   Quoted in: https://time.com/5908983/president-elect-joe-biden-vows-to-usher-in-a-time-to-heal-in-america/ (accessed September 13, 2023).

interactions. For example, a *promise* only works if both representatives and constituents understand it *as a promise* and understand *what is being promised* (see Mansbridge, 2003, p. 525), and the same is true for, say, an apology that a representative offers to constituents (e.g., for not acting the way initially promised).

Communicative acts without speech. This leads us to the second type of communicative acts that political representatives may perform, acts that are communicative but do not involve speech. It is uncontroversial that actions can be communicative without being speech acts: as much has been said about *voting* (e.g., Fearon, 1999, p. 59) or *protesting* (e.g., Medina, 2023), and it is not difficult to imagine a range of other kinds of nonspeech acts or activities that communicate something about how a (would-be) representative would like to be seen by other citizens. At this general level, we may think of what Warren (2017, pp. 45–51) terms "generic democratic practices," such as *recognizing*, *exiting*, or *joining*. Visible acts of *recognizing* others can be nonverbal in that they may be reduced gestures such as handshakes or hugs (think of the innumerable images of politicians shaking hands with others, whom they thereby "recognize" as equals of sorts). *Exiting* can equally be communicative without involving speech, for example, when representatives leave a room out of protest against a particular speaker. *Joining* may simply involve partaking in a public march or manifestation to signal solidarity with a particular group or cause, just as New Zealand's Prime Minister Jacinda Ardern did when she publicly met members of the Muslim community of Christchurch after the Christchurch terrorist attack in March 2019, wearing a headscarf (see Figure 4). This could for instance be interpreted as a promise on the part of the government to stand with a particular minority community that is facing real threats to their collective security. All of these categories of action communicate to citizens something regarding how the (would-be) representative in question would like to be seen by them, who the (would-be) representative seeks to speak and act for, and so on.

Obviously, *images* often play a central role in all of this: it is through images of certain speech-free communicative acts that a larger audience of (would-be) constituents can become aware of the fact that (would-be) representatives have performed those acts. Indeed, since the wider public will – contrary to Mansbridge's normative demands – only rarely have direct contact with (would-be) representatives, and hence be confined to the role of "spectators" who observe what (would-be) representatives do from a distance (on this, see Green, 2010), such images are important for establishing and maintaining representative relationships. Usually, these images are disseminated via traditional or social media (the exemplary picture in Figure 4 is taken from Twitter/X), and they may be still

Figure 4 Example of a communicative act without speech
Note: Picture reprinted with permission from Christchurch City Council.

or moving images. And often, perhaps typically, images of (would-be) representatives are carefully curated by teams of (social) media experts who try to make sure that the (would-be) representative is presented to the public, as well as to more specific audiences, in a particular fashion. This is crucial because it is about *exercising control over which kinds of communicative acts reach larger audiences in the first place.*

Of course, communicative acts without speech can also be disseminated *without* images, most notably through written or spoken reports of the act. Think, for example, of a newspaper article mentioning that "politician X was one of the few within her party to vote against motion Y in parliament," or TV news reporting that "politician Y has refused to shake hands with the leader of party P." Here, no images are needed to transport the message; the act fulfils its communicative function through others speaking about it.

Table 2 summarizes the two kinds of communicative acts that (would-be) representatives perform in order to enact a particular representative role. Before proceeding to investigate how citizens might evaluate representatives' communicative acts, however, one potential worry must be addressed. This is that there is an almost infinite universe of verbal and nonverbal communicative acts that may be relevant for the constitution and maintenance of representative relationships. How, then, should we decide which communicative acts to study? Our response is that there is no good theoretical reason for restricting our focus to

Table 2 Two kinds of communicative acts

	Speech acts	**Communicative acts without speech**
Description	Utterances made by (would-be) representatives that are meant to perform the function of conjuring up a particular image of themselves	Actions performed by (would-be) representatives that do not involve speech but are meant to instill, reinforce, or resonate with, the image that the (would-be) representative would like to conjure up
Indicative examples	Promises of what a (would-be) representative will do or *be* once (re)elected; apologies to constituents for not delivering what was promised, etc.	(Visibly) voting for a particular policy; joining a public march or manifestation; exiting a debate in protest, etc.

any more limited range of communicative acts. Researchers should be open to studying all sorts of different communicative acts, provided that they can be empirically studied. One way of focusing the analysis that is consistent with our citizen-centered approach would be to concentrate on types of communicative acts that citizens (appear to) pay most attention to. But this is just one possible way of limiting the scope of possibly relevant units of analysis, and it presupposes, rather demandingly, a sound understanding of the citizen perspective.

3.3 Core Components of Representation II: No Representation without Citizens' Evaluations!

Let us return to the two components of political representation that constitute the core of our theoretical framework: (1) *representatives' communicative acts*, and (2) *citizens' evaluations of representatives' communicative acts*. And recall that these two component parts are derived from our definition of representation as a *relationship between citizens and politicians that arises when citizens positively evaluate communicative acts that politicians perform in their capacity as holders of certain institutionalized roles.* This definition already indicates that citizens' evaluations of (would-be) representatives' communicative acts are absolutely crucial for representative relationships to come into existence in the first place. (Would-be) representatives may attempt to communicate a range of different things to their (would-be) constituents, but only if their communicative acts are seen, heard or read about, and evaluated positively by (would-be) constituents does a representative relationship emerge. "Evaluated positively" here means that (would-be) constituents affirm what (would-be) representatives are doing. Relating this to our previous examples, (would-be) constituents might think, "Thankfully Joe Biden is trying to overcome the toxic polarization plaguing our country!" or "I'm glad that Jacinda Ardern is taking a stand for the Muslim community of New Zealand!"

Citizens' evaluations of (would-be) representatives' communicative acts are so important from an interactive constructivist perspective because interactive constructivism conceives political representation as a two-way relationship. Citizens are treated not as passive recipients of (would-be) representatives' communicative acts, but as agents who can *directly* (e.g., questioning a would-be representative in a personal encounter at a campaign rally) or, perhaps more likely, *indirectly* (e.g., reading a newspaper article about certain communicative acts performed by would-be representatives and then forming some evaluative views on those acts) engage with those communicative acts. They can engage *individually* with those communications (e.g., reflecting on the relevance of them for oneself) or discuss them *collectively* with others – or even with the (would-be) representative if given the opportunity. They can also decide to ignore certain communicative acts, but insofar as this is a deliberate decision, it also amounts to engagement.

Interactive constructivists usually commit to a further idea in this connection: the idea that citizens' positive evaluation of (would-be) representatives' communicative acts not only establishes a representative relationship, but also renders that relationship – at least provisionally – *democratically legitimate* (see, e.g., Saward, 2018, p. 288). This way of thinking about the democratic legitimacy of representative relationships puts the citizen perspective front and center. Saward (2010, p. 146), whom we have cited throughout as a key advocate of the interactive constructivist camp, suggests that this way of approaching the question of legitimacy is the *most democratic* way:

> Given the burdens of judgment and the extraordinarily difficult epistemo-
> logical issues involved in forging independent criteria of legitimacy, [it is]
> crucial ... that we address relevant constituencies and audiences and say:
> "It is up to you to judge. From a democratic standpoint, it is your job to
> adjudicate on the democratic credentials of representative claims,

particularly those which seek to invoke you as a member of a constituency, making allegations about your character or wishes in the process." There may be varied means of assessing ... democratic legitimacy ... but this ... is the democrats' way.

None of this is to say that scholars of representation must remain uncritical about citizens' evaluations of representatives' communicative acts, or that plausible additional evaluative standards cannot be developed without compromising one's democratic commitments (we think, in fact, that developing such standards is an important task for future research). Nor, indeed, do we wish to suggest that a representative whose communicative acts are positively evaluated by a citizen will be regarded by that citizen as legitimately representing them in *all matters of concern*. However, not least because we are venturing into new territory theoretically and empirically, we will for now limit ourselves to the more minimalist standard of legitimacy that Saward proposes as a working conception of how representative relationships may acquire legitimacy. If one believes, as Sabl (2015, p. 255) puts it, that "what ordinary people value is worth a provisional respect," this minimalist standard is not a bad starting point.

3.3.1 Sources and Constructions of Citizens' Representation Preferences

How structured and predictable should we expect citizens' evaluations of representatives' communicative acts to be? Clearly, a set of particular circumstances, such as the time, place, framing, prominence, how commentators interpret the communicative act, and so forth, will influence how citizens evaluate a communicative act. However, we posit that citizens also hold some *general preferences for how they want to be represented* that are rather fixed, at least in the short run (e.g., in cross-sectional analyses). These preferences give structure to the evaluation of communicative acts aimed at representation. Most citizens probably rarely engage in rational information processing regarding how exactly they want to be represented, piecing together their observations of the political world with their self-observed interests. Yet they may still rather consistently know what they want from representation based on individual predispositions and the use of cues or heuristics (see, e.g., Leeper & Slothuus, 2014; Lupia, 1994; Lupia & McCubbins, 1998). Our argument is not that such preferences for representation are necessarily rational, competent, or enlightened. We only suggest that there is some degree of structure, and potentially also, "constraint" in citizens' attitudes toward representation (Converse, 1964). This is the case because questions about how one wants to be represented relate to *fundamental values, group affiliations and political identities* people hold, and opinion formation on representation is influenced by *cognitive abilities and biases* – just as it is the case with many other political preferences:

- *Values* such as authority, religiosity, or public order may shape my understanding of how politicians should behave in representing, for instance, as authority figures taking care of public affairs rather than mediators between myself and the political sphere.
- *Partisanship* is likely a strong source of citizens' representation preferences. The vast majority of democratic politicians are members of a political party, maintaining different types of connections to their party, and citizens' attachment to and alienation from parties will shape how they want the politician to represent them. Partisanship may also influence the extent to which citizens want politicians to only represent themselves and co-partisans as opposed to viewing representation as a cross-partisan endeavor.
- *Group-based identities*, such as attachment to the nation, a social class, or an ethnic group, comprise another important source of representation preferences. Depending on which groups I feel I belong to, I may want the politician to focus their communicative acts on appealing to these groups and include them in representation, while I may not care about or even desire the exclusion of other groups (e.g., where groups are polarized in society).
- *Cognitive abilities* and *political sophistication* will also define expectations toward representation. For instance, if I am (or at least feel) competent myself to decide which policies are in my interests, I may view a "good representative" to simply amplify my views at the political stage, whereas I may prefer the representative to take care of all issues and decide themselves if I am not well versed in politics.

What these sources of representation preferences have in common is that they are all clearly *prior to evaluations of representative acts*, anchoring and giving structure to citizens' representation preferences. Individuals' fundamental values, identities, and abilities are rarely changed through communicative acts by politicians, especially not in the short run. Hence, these sources provide some exogenous, relatively fixed roots of representation preferences. This is not to say that citizens' evaluations of single communicative acts will only (or even mostly) derive from these factors or that politicians cannot influence what kind of representation citizens prefer. Given our commitment to interactive constructivism, we account for the possibility that politicians can influence citizens' evaluations of their acts through priming, framing, and persuasion. Elite influence on citizens' political preferences is well documented (e.g., Bisgaard & Slothuus, 2018; Leeper & Slothuus, 2014). However, there is also ample evidence for the limits of elite influence on preferences, especially when competition between political opponents gives rise to different positions on a particular issue, and when the availability of issue-relevant information incentivizes systematic information processing (e.g., Amsalem & Zoizner, 2020; Bullock, 2011; Druckman, 2004).

Indeed, if – as some radical-democratic constructivists claim (e.g., Disch, 2011, 2021) – representation were *only* about representatives' discursively eliciting constituencies and, by extension, framing their preferences, then the concept of citizens' representation preferences would make little sense. All of citizens' representation preferences would be produced by representatives. If we accept an interactive-constructivist ontology, on the other hand, it remains meaningful to speak of citizens' representation preferences. This is because interactive constructivism does not rule out that citizens hold views that are at least partially derived from predispositions that exhibit some stability over time and cannot be reduced to politicians' efforts at mobilization, such as particular values or group identities.

3.4 Dimensions of Analysis

Every communicative act potentially contains different kinds of information that citizens might react to and use to evaluate the act. This raises the analytical question of which of these kinds of information we should analyze when studying political representation. To address this issue, we use contemporary representation theory as a guide. This work has rarely (if ever) been motivated by the question of which aspects of representation are important to citizens, but it provides us with a conceptual starting point from which research can begin (with the important caveat that the conceptual apparatus may be revised at a later stage).

Specifically, we suggest analyzing communicative acts on up to six different dimensions, relating to six different kinds of information contained in these acts. The first two dimensions, *substantive* and *descriptive* representation, we take from Pitkin (1967), whose conceptions of representation inform most quantitative-empirical work on representation. We do not include Pitkin's conception of "*formalistic* representation," since its two subdimensions – the authorization and accountability processes through which a politician attains, remains, and is replaced in their institutionalized position – are fixed by a country's specific electoral institutions. The main variations in formalistic representation therefore occur between representatives holding different institutionalized positions within a country (e.g., a president vs. an MP) and between countries (e.g., a party-list MP in the Netherlands and a directly elected House Representative in the United States). But we expect less individual-level variation, which is our analytical focus.

Nor do we include *symbolic* representation. This dimension refers to citizens' attribution of symbolic meaning to a representative (e.g., a minister symbolizes "law and order" or a president symbolizes "the nation"). Conceptually, these are one-way attributions of meaning, which may include the attribution of meaning to an inanimate object like a flag, thereby expanding the idea of representation beyond our relational approach, in which representatives are always agents and not objects. This is difficult to capture by our conceptual toolbox, which treats representatives' communicative acts and citizens' evaluations of the latter as primary units of analysis as well as emphasizes the interactive nature of representation. However, we do think that the six dimensions presented next can capture some of the things entailed in symbolic representation. For example, a politician's likelihood to be seen as standing for the "nation" will likely be influenced by their propensity to justify policies as serving the good of the entire political community (we call this "republican justification").[6]

In addition, we suggest analyzing four further dimensions that can be derived from key theoretical innovations in the theory of representation (e.g., Mansbridge, 2003; Rehfeld, 2009; Saward, 2010). We call these dimensions *surrogation, justification, personalization,* and *responsiveness*, respectively. We have previously introduced these dimensions, arguing that they track those aspects of representation that theoretical scholars have recently paid most attention to and that at the same time are feasibly operationalizable with quantitative methods (Wolkenstein & Wratil, 2021). We now introduce each dimension in greater detail, illustrate with examples how they can be salient in a variety of different types of communicative acts performed by politicians, and discuss what factors likely shape citizens' representation preferences regarding the dimensions. Note already that each communicative act may contain elements that make it relevant to none, one, two, three, or – indeed – all six of the dimensions.

3.4.1 Substantive Representation

First, starting with the *substantive* dimension of representation, this refers to those elements of communicative acts that provide cues about whether a *politician advances the policy preferences* of citizens.[7] This can take numerous forms – from a campaign poster that advocates for a higher minimum wage,

---

[6] In addition, in many cases – especially where symbolic meanings are very subjective – it is hard to study those dimensions with quantitative approaches that aim at reliability and intersubjective validity. However, we are excited about new work that tries to operationalize symbolic dimensions of representation through quantitative approaches.

[7] Note that we focus on "policy preferences" instead of "preferences" in general, as we think that substantive representation has been mostly understood in this way in empirical research and as it helpfully substantiates the concept.

to voting for a ban of abortion in the legislature, to posting pictures of one's participation in a Fridays for Future protest on social media. The core of the substantive dimension is an explicit or implicit cue that the politician holds, and acts in a way consistent with, a particular position on a policy issue. This cue can become constitutive of representation to the extent that a citizen approves of the politician's position on the policy issue. The prominence of the issue in politicians' communications and the personal importance of the issue to citizens influence how likely the communicative act is to bring about a representative relationship.

Our understanding of the substantive dimension focuses on what we consider the conceptual core of Pitkin's (1967) original definition, that is, representation as "acting in the interest of the represented" (p. 209). We are not concerned here with why this acting occurs (which may be unobservable, e.g., in the case of a representative's intrinsic motivation to act in a particular way). Some empirical scholars have understood the substantive dimension in much more specific terms, often relying on the second part of the previous quote, where Pitkin notes that representatives act "in a manner responsive to [the constituents]" (p. 209). This notion of "responsiveness" is often conceived in dynamic terms and attributed to incentives flowing from elections. For example, Stimson et al. (1995, p. 545) write, "[w]hen politicians perceive public opinion change, they adapt their behavior to please their constituency and, accordingly, enhance their chances of reelection." Substantive representation, on this view, means that representatives act in the interest of the represented by dynamically updating their views about the interests of the represented and changing policy accordingly to forestall electoral sanctions at the ballot box. Our argument is that such notions of election-induced responsiveness are not necessarily part of how Pitkin conceptualized substantive representation. Pitkin neither specifies how much responsiveness is needed for "good" substantive representation, nor does she identify particular mechanisms that should ensure that representatives act in the interests of the represented. Given that Pitkin (1967, p. 209) envisages representatives to "act independently" based on their own "discretion and judgment," she in fact leaves room for varying levels of responsiveness to constituents and for other mechanisms beyond electoral sanctioning that may bring about substantive representation. So, we separate the core of substantive representation (i.e., advancing the policy preferences of constituents) from any notion of "responsiveness," which we define in a more specific way as an independent dimension of representation.

An example of a communicative act with an explicit substantive dimension is depicted in the campaign poster of the populist and radical right-wing Freedom Party of Austria (FPÖ) in Figure 5. The party's current chairman, Herbert Kickl, is depicted in a waterproof jacket with the slogan "Fortress

Figure 5 Example of substantive dimension in communicative act – Freedom
Party of Austria campaign poster (2023)
Note: FPÖ election poster from 2023, picture licensed by IMAGO images.

Austria – Close the borders – Guarantee security." In the background there is
also a hand with the imprint "stop asylum." The poster thus clearly communicates that Kickl and the FPÖ as a party want to close the borders to immigrants
and stop asylum seekers' immigration into Austria. These are obvious, quite
specific policy positions that are contained in this communicative act.
However, some may be more subtle and read into the poster only by some
viewers, think of "building a fence or wall around Austria," "spending more
money on border surveillance," or "closing the borders to a specific group of
migrants only." These are nuances that many quantitative approaches to
analyzing such acts may not be able to capture reliably. But these limitations
should not distract from the fact that the act communicates specific policy
positions that can be extracted to some extent (e.g., through human coding or
quantitative text analysis).

Citizens are generally assumed to strongly value substantive representation
(see, e.g., Costa, 2020; Harden, 2015). However, one reason why citizens'
evaluation of substantive representation may vary is that citizens often lack

clear-cut policy preferences across multiple policy domains due to a lack of knowledge or competence (e.g., Achen & Bartels, 2017). This suggests that *political sophistication* is a key source of citizens' general preferences for substantive representation. Highly sophisticated citizens tend to be more educated and informed about as well as interested and active in politics. This also makes them vote more based on policy issue positions, at least where issues are "hard" issues, that is, technical, pragmatic, and short-lived (Carmines & Stimson, 1980; Kim et al., 2005). In contrast, less sophisticated citizens typically have weaker preferences for substantive representation, as they may, for instance, focus more on other dimensions of representation that demand less sophistication to be grasped (e.g., the descriptive or justification dimensions). In fact, previous work has found that the importance of policy issue representation for citizens increases with education, income, and employment – three factors correlated with political sophistication (Harden, 2015; Lapinski et al., 2016). A related expectation is that less sophisticated citizens will place more importance on communicative acts where the substantive dimension of representation depends less on their own personal preferences because it is obvious that it would be in every constituent's interest, such as certain valence issues. Prominent examples include the allocation of funding to the district (e.g., pork-barrel politics), or the performance of constituency service and case work. Hence, preferences for substantive representation should be strongest among the highly sophisticated, whereas the less sophisticated are expected to have weaker preferences, especially where policy issues are "hard" and policy preferences are not uniform.

3.4.2 Descriptive Representation

Second, the *descriptive* dimension refers to elements of the communicative act that provide information about descriptive *characteristics of the politician and their related life experiences*, such as gender, age, ethnicity, social class, education, or a migratory background. In many communicative acts, the descriptive dimension is contained in the visual layer: representatives may dress as and look like women, they may look to be 60–70 years of age, and may have a skin color that looks like they are of Latino descent. But information about such characteristics can also be conveyed in representatives' speech, when they speak of themselves "as a woman" or "as a gay man," emphasizing certain characteristics of their being and potentially connecting it with experiences (e.g., "I always had to fight for myself harder than others"). For Pitkin (1967, p. 60), descriptive representation simply arises to the extent that the collective of representatives accurately resembles constituents on these

characteristics: "a representative body is distinguished by an accurate correspondence or resemblance to what it represents, by reflecting without distortion."
We here apply the idea of descriptive representation to the individual level as
well: each representative can resemble a single constituent to varying degrees
on descriptive characteristics, which will impact on whether the communicative
act establishes a representation relationship (also see Mansbridge, 1999).

Notice that, for Pitkin (1967), descriptive representation is about representatives' accurately representing key descriptive "facts" about the represented; so,
if there are 50 percent women among the represented, there should be 50 percent
women among the representatives. Descriptive representation therefore leaves
little interpretive latitude. In the ideal, it provides an unbiased map of information about the represented. Now, being committed to constructivism at a general
theoretical level, we do not necessarily assume that descriptive characteristics
are always *objective*, fixed facts; rather, we assume that they can be *constructed*
through speech acts and nonspeech practice. Since representation comes into
being through the positive evaluation of communicative acts by citizens, it is
their *own "mental" construction* of their personal characteristics and that of
the representatives that is crucial. Someone may be a man by prevailing legal
definitions, but if they have constructed their own gender identity as a "trans-
woman" or simply a "woman," it is the representation of this very identity by a
representative that may lead to descriptive representation – not the representation of a male identity following prevailing legal definitions of who counts as
male (or female).

Figure 6 provides a picture of US House Representative Alexandria Ocasio-
Cortez, when holding a speech in Congress on 23 July 2020. It was a speech that
made the Democratic Ocasio-Cortez famous, as she powerfully addressed sexist
remarks levied against her by another Republican House Representative.
Ocasio-Cortez said:

> In front of reporters, Representative Yoho called me, and I quote, "A fucking
> bitch." These are the words that Representative Yoho levied against a con-
> gresswoman. A congresswoman that not only represents New York's 14th
> congressional district, but every congresswoman and every woman in this
> country because all of us have had to deal with this in some form, some way,
> some shape, at some point in our lives.

Ocasio-Cortez clearly mobilizes her identity as a (congress)woman and follows
up with a representative claim that, in her remarks about the sexist slur uttered
by her colleague, she is representing "every woman in this country." Moreover,
she invokes shared life experiences of the descriptive group of "women" that
she wants to represent, later also sharing personal examples of it: "I have

Figure 6 Example of descriptive dimension in communicative act – Alexandria
Ocasio-Cortez' speech in the US Congress (2020)
Note: "Rep. Alexandria Ocasio-Cortez speaking to attendees at a rally for Bernie
Sanders in Council Bluffs, Iowa" by Matt A.J., used under CC BY 2.0.

encountered words uttered by Mr. Yoho and men uttering the same words as Mr.
Yoho, while I was being harassed in restaurants. I have tossed men out of bars
that have used language like Mr. Yoho's, and I have encountered this type of
harassment riding the subway in New York City." It is exactly this attempt to
evoke a group defined by certain descriptive characteristics through mentioning
shared experiences that is distinctive for how the descriptive dimension may be
expressed through representatives' communicative acts.

Citizens may vary greatly in whether they value descriptive representation,
however. Some may be indifferent toward it, or even reject it. We argue that a key
source of variation in general preferences toward descriptive representation are
marginalized group identities. Identifying with a marginalized group should lead
to a strong preference for descriptive representation, whereas belonging to a
dominant, majority group may even be associated with a rejection of descriptive
representation. Due to their (historical) subordination, members of marginalized
groups (e.g., women, blacks in the United States, etc.) may harbor significant
distrust in the capacity of politicians belonging to a dominant group to represent
them (e.g., Mansbridge, 1999). In turn, citizens identifying with the dominant
group may be less skeptical that someone will represent them, even if
politicians do not resemble them descriptively or emphasize their descriptive

identity in their communicative acts. The difference in trusting to be represented is thus based on the positive vs. negative experiences marginalized vs. dominant groups have made with representation.

One further factor rendering descriptive representation more important to citizens with marginalized group identities is that, if they were to put little weight on this dimension of representation, they might risk ending up with very few or no descriptively congruent representatives in institutionalized political positions. In contrast, majority group politicians will always fill up a part of the positions, even if citizens identifying with such groups do not care much about descriptive representation. Some research has shown that citizens often do not care much about descriptive representation itself, but rather treat it as a cue for substantive representation wherever they have no information whether someone represents them substantively (Arnesen et al., 2019). Hayes and Hibbing (2017) even find that – in some contexts – the dominant group of white US citizens negatively evaluates their own descriptive representation and instead prefers a stronger representation of blacks. In turn, especially research based on qualitative interviewing has documented marginalized groups' comparatively strong and fine-grained preference for descriptive representation (e.g., de Jong & Mügge, 2023; Schildkraut, 2013).

3.4.3 Surrogation

Third, the *surrogation* dimension of representation refers to instances where a politician's communicative acts successfully mobilize citizens who have neither directly nor indirectly voted for the politician – there is a *representative* relationship, but no *electoral* relationship. There are two sub-forms of surrogation. What we call *territorial surrogation* is defined by Mansbridge (2003, p. 522) as "representation by a representative with whom one has no electoral relationship—that is, a representative in another district" for whom one cannot vote. This means that territorial surrogation is a feature of *any* representative relationship that spans across electoral districts, where a politician was not on the ballot paper that a citizen was entitled to use in elections. To illustrate, the quote by Ocasio-Cortez we just discussed also entails a dimension of territorial surrogation. Having been elected in New York's 14th congressional district, she still claims that she represents "every woman in this country" – more than one hundred million of which only a tiny fraction lives and votes in her district.

The second sub-form of surrogate representation, *partisan surrogation*, occurs where politicians claim to represent citizens who have cast a vote for an opponent party or opponent party candidate (Wolkenstein & Wratil, 2021). In

Section 4.2, we presented a tweet by Joe Biden that has a clear element of partisan surrogation in his claim that "[w]hether you voted for me or against me, I will represent you." Here, *all* people, who "voted for me or against me" that Biden is addressing, had a chance of voting for him – on their ballot paper in each state – but many decided to vote for someone else. There is *only* partisan and *no* territorial surrogation in this example. However, in the Ocasio-Cortez example *both* sub-forms are present, since "every woman in this country" also includes those (inside and outside her district) who have not voted for her or another Democratic candidate.

It is important to realize that surrogation – like no other of our dimensions of analysis – is to some extent predefined by political institutions. In a national context, territorial surrogation can only exist where an electoral system tier is divided into different geographical districts (e.g., in single-member district systems). In contrast, in systems with a single nation-wide multi-member district (e.g., the Netherlands), territorial surrogation is not defined. However, note that territorial surrogation can always occur on a transnational level, where politicians in one country claim to represent citizens in another country that could never have voted for them (see the example of Annalena Baerbock later in this section). Partisan surrogation, in turn, is shaped by the party system. A higher number of parties creates more opportunities for partisan surrogation, especially if several parties build a "block" and see each other as partners; independent, nonpartisan candidates (e.g., running for president) reduce options for partisan surrogation.

Figure 7 provides one further example of territorial (more explicit) and partisan (more implicit) surrogation. It shows a tweet by Terry Reintke, a Member of the European Parliament, who focuses large parts of her work on the fight for fundamental rights (in particular, of LGBTQI citizens), from January 2022. Members of the European Parliament are elected by national or regional party lists or by single transferable vote in each EU country. Reintke was re-elected to the European Parliament on a national party list of the German Greens in 2019. Hence, all voters who indirectly voted for her through the party list were EU citizens resident in Germany. By stating that she fights for fundamental rights of EU citizens "whether they live in Spain, Poland or elsewhere," she claims to represent citizens who are in no electoral relationship with her, because neither her party nor herself were on the ballot paper in either Spain or Poland. This is *territorial surrogation across countries*. More implicitly, one could also interpret some claim of partisan surrogation, since "EU citizens" also includes those that have not voted for the Greens, though it is not this sub-form of surrogation that she has decided to make salient in this tweet.

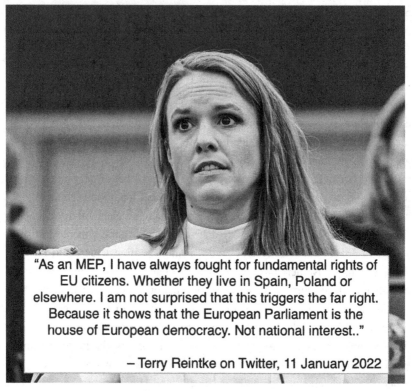

"As an MEP, I have always fought for fundamental rights of EU citizens. Whether they live in Spain, Poland or elsewhere. I am not surprised that this triggers the far right. Because it shows that the European Parliament is the house of European democracy. Not national interest.."

– Terry Reintke on Twitter, 11 January 2022

Figure 7 Example of surrogation dimension in communicative act – Terry Reintke's tweet on EU citizens' fundamental rights (2022)
Note: Unnamed picture of Terry Reintke by European Parliament, used under CC BY 4.0/Text box has been added by the authors.

Generally, citizens are expected to prefer representative relationships based on direct electoral accountability of the representative over surrogate relationships. Elections are a key component of most people's understanding of democracy (e.g., Ferrín & Kriesi, 2016), and attitudes toward representation are likely to be in part derived from people's very attitudes toward democracy. That is, people may use their understanding of "good democracy" as a cue for what "good representation" is, and if they consider elections central to democracy, they may thus conclude it should involve representatives one elected. Of course, in reality not everyone can be represented by someone they elected. Elections create losers whose voters still need representation and sometimes the "best" representative one can think of is running in a different district. In this light, we argue that *education* should be a key antecedent of preferences for surrogate representation (see, e.g., Harden, 2015; Lapinski et al., 2016). Whereas citizens with lower levels of education may rely on the cognitive shortcut that *representation must involve direct electoral accountability,* more educated citizens may have cognized that this is not attainable and so entertain the possibility of, or even welcome, surrogate representation. Moreover, given that a large literature argues that affluent and highly educated people receive better representation than others (e.g., Gilens, 2012; Schakel & Van Der Pas, 2021), those with lower education and income may also prefer direct electoral accountability more to ensure a representative adheres to their wishes. In turn, the higher educated may be fine with surrogate representation, as they may (reasonably) expect that representatives usually act in their interests.

Regarding partisan surrogation specifically, we also expect the strength of *partisanship* to shape citizens' preferences. Citizens without or with weak partisanship may not care much about whether a politician is from the party they voted for, whereas strong partisans may find it unimaginable and unacceptable to be represented by someone with a different partisan identity. Partisanship acts as a social identity, can animate strong emotions against out-partisans and bias political perceptions (Bartels, 2002; Iyengar et al., 2019). Strong partisans, therefore, may not only dislike representation by politicians from other parties, but also filter out or unfairly evaluate any information that might suggest that a partisan surrogate representative is acting in their interests. To our knowledge, almost no work to date has studied citizens' preferences toward the surrogation dimension of representation (but see Blumenau et al. 2024).

3.4.4 Justification

Fourth, the *justification* dimension of representation is concerned with the *declared aims behind politicians' actions,* as expressed in representatives' communicative acts. While politicians can use a plethora of aims to justify their actions, the theoretical debate has focused on the distinction between whether aims are justified as serving the good of the whole citizenry (*republican aims*), or the particularistic good(s) of some societal group(s) (*pluralist aims*) (Rehfeld, 2009). For our purposes, and in line with an interactive constructivist ontology, it is central which aims a politician claims to advance – not which aims are advanced in some "objective" sense of the term, as in aims that serve some groups' "objective" material interests. This is also the dominant understanding of practices of justification in the theoretical literature (see White & Ypi, 2016, Chap. 3). This means, for instance, that a politician may justify their support for policies that appear evidently targeted to particularistic groups, such as unemployment benefits or a tax cut for top earners, by invoking the public good of "building a just society" or "unleashing economic growth for all." Similarly, an action that may appear aimed at the good of society, such as imposing a lockdown during an otherwise uncontrollable phase of a pandemic, can be communicated as "protecting the elderly and sick," focusing on the good of some groups.

Justification is the dimension of analysis that is most salient in speech acts as opposed to communicative acts without speech. The very idea of "justifying one's acting" is calling for an utterance. When we want somebody to justify, to explain themselves, we usually are not content if they remain silent and just leave us with a gesture, for instance. In fact, we believe that communicative acts without any speech or text will rarely contain clearly identifiable information regarding the justification of actions. Sometimes speech acts with a justification element can be reinforced through other nonspeech elements. Think of a US president who justifies their immigration policies with the good they bring for immigrant communities in front of the Statue of Liberty – which is widely seen as the American symbol for acknowledging immigrant communities' contribution. Likewise, think of a national health minister who visits a clinic with COVID-19 patients when justifying their COVID-19 mitigation policies in terms of the good of the sick and elderly who suffer most from the disease. Still, speech acts are undeniably core to the justification dimension of political representation.

One example of justification that neatly illustrates the focus on "claimed" rather than any "objective" aims is provided by Hungarian Prime Minister Viktor Orbán in a radio interview in September 2023,[8] in which he extensively speaks about family policy (a topic of high priority to Orbán and his party):

> The truth is that, when I look at European politics from the point of view of families, I can see who cares about families, who wants to support families, and who wants to help young people have the children they want. I see who it is that thinks in terms of the homeland and nation, and who knows that the existence or non-existence of children is linked to the existence or non-existence of one's homeland. [...] This is why the Government's aim is to ensure that those who have children are better off financially than those who don't.

Here, a policy that to some will appear extremely particularistic in focus – making people with children financially better off than those without – is justified in the name of a republican aim, addressing the good of society, of guaranteeing the "existence [...] of one's homeland."

As far as we know, almost no work has addressed citizens' preferences for justification thus far (but see Blumenau et al. 2024). We conjecture that one key

---

[8] Kossuth Radio program "Good Morning Hungary," September 15, 2023; https://abouthungary.hu/speeches-and-remarks/prime-minister-viktor-orban-on-the-kossuth-radio-programme-good-morning-hungary-65082fc6a4b73.

source for whether citizens like or dislike politicians to advance pluralist vs. republican justifications could be the *scope of their social identity*. If individuals' self-conceptions include a social group that encompasses many in society or beyond that society (e.g., if they see themselves as "citizen of the country," "citizen of Europe/the world"), they should value republican justifications referring to the good of the whole. In turn, if individuals mainly consider themselves to be part of smaller groups (e.g., "farmers," "pensioners," or "single mums/dads"), we expect them to appreciate pluralist justifications that focus on the good of a part of society. Note that many analytical perspectives on the scope of personal identity draw attention to differences between those who see themselves as part of the nation and those whose identity transcends national contexts (e.g., Hooghe & Marks, 2004; Zollinger, 2024). In contrast, in terms of justification, the most salient difference is between identification with societal sub-groups vs. society, the nation, and the world as a whole.

3.4.5 Personalization

Fifth, the *personalization* dimension of representation refers to elements of communicative acts that frame what we call the *relationship of dependence between a politician and their party*. Some politicians try to emancipate themselves from their party through their communicative acts by voting or speaking out publicly against the party line or leadership, as well as by emphasizing their personal qualities and background to voters, treating their party affiliation as secondary.[9] Conversely, other politicians may closely toe the party line, justify and explain party leaders' decisions in public, and portray themselves as "agents" of the party as a larger collective political endeavor. Broadly speaking, the personalization dimension has two components: *positioning toward the party* (e.g., a politician attacks their party leadership) and *developing a personal profile* (e.g., a politician portrays themselves as a strongly independent mind). The relationship between politicians and their party can become a constitutive feature of representation, where citizens want their representatives to act more like "party rebels," or alternatively, like "party soldiers," and these preferences are mirrored in politicians' communicative acts.

Personalization is a dimension of analysis that does not figure in any clear-cut way in recent work on representation theory (e.g., Mansbridge, 2003; Rehfeld, 2009; Saward, 2010), not least because *political parties* have been all but completely under-theorized in this body of literature. This absence is strange. After all, parties were seen as indispensable for effective political representation

---

[9] Notice that there may, for this reason, be a close connection between the descriptive and personalization dimensions of representation.

for the larger part of the twentieth century (e.g., Kelsen, 2013; Schattschneider, 1942). And although they have often been said to be in crisis today (Invernizzi-Accetti & Wolkenstein, 2017; Mair, 2013), they have established themselves so firmly as a central institutional feature of most, if not all, developed democracies that it would be absurd to theorize them out of the picture in a conceptual discussion of political representation (Katz & Mair, 2009; Van Biezen, 2012). Hence, we think it is important to consider each communicative act of representation a politician performs also with regard to how it positions the politician vis-à-vis their party.

To illustrate what communicative acts about personalization might look like in practice, consider Figure 8. It depicts twenty-one British Conservative MPs who defied their own party's instructions, when voting with the opposition parties to make Parliament consider the so-called Benn Act that sought to prevent a "no deal" departure of the United Kingdom from the EU in September 2019. Within hours after their vote against their party, the Conservatives withdrew the whip from the twenty-one MPs, who were now sitting as independents in the House of Commons. This "rebellion" was arguably one of the most consequential acts of personalization against a party in modern British history, eventually triggering a snap general election and an extension of the UK's withdrawal date from the EU. While in this case the MPs' voting behavior and its consequences by themselves

Figure 8 Example of personalization dimension in communicative act – 21 British
Conservative MPs who voted against their own government on Brexit (2019)
Note: All portraits retrieved from UK House of Commons, used under CC BY 3.0/
Collage created by Laura Pfisterer.

communicated their distancing from their party, politicians often also use speech acts to explain their positioning vis-à-vis the party through a vote (see, e.g., Duell et al., 2023). MP Justine Greening did so as well in this instance, when announcing on the same day that she would not stand as a Conservative candidate again: "[I]t's clear to me that whoever is next elected to represent our constituency, which voted over 70% Remain, they will similarly need to put our community views on Brexit first, ahead of any conflicting party interest" (on Twitter, now X, 3 September 2019). Here, Greening explains her defection from the party in terms of representing her constituents' views on the Brexit policy issue (i.e., substantive representation).

Research on citizens' evaluations of personalization has overwhelmingly reported a strong general preference for party-independent representatives (e.g., Bøggild, 2020; Bøggild & Pedersen, 2020; Campbell et al., 2019). The most likely explanation for this is that citizens use politicians' acts of distancing themselves from their party as a cue for the representative's valence. For instance, Duell et al. (2024) experimentally show that rebellious MPs who vote against their party are seen as more "independent," "honest," and holding "strong personal convictions" – which are all positive valence traits from the perspective of most voters. Despite the general endorsement of party independence, however, we expect citizens' preferences for personalization to vary on the individual level by the strength of *partisanship*. While party independence can be electorally beneficial for the politicians themselves, a disunified image of the party in public has been shown to be damaging to the electoral fortunes of the party (e.g., Greene & Haber, 2015; Lehrer et al., 2024). Strong partisans should care more about the electoral prospects of their party than citizens with weak or no partisanship, such as swing voters. Indeed, Campbell et al. (2019) marshal some evidence that the preference for independent MPs is stronger among less partisan citizens than among those with strong partisan identities. But note that in their results even strong partisans prefer relatively strong levels of personalization over party loyalism.

3.4.6 Responsiveness

Sixth, our final dimension of analysis, *responsiveness*, is concerned with elements of a communicative act that signal the *politician's sensitivity to electoral sanctions*. On an explicit level, some politicians may assert their sensitivity to electoral sanctions by invoking popular sovereignty (e.g., "in a democracy, the voter has the last word and therefore I always listen and respond to what voters want") or stressing the practical necessity of re-election for realizing certain political goals (e.g., "I can only change society if I am re-elected"). Other politicians may reject the idea of responsiveness by reference to their own principles or some higher mission that voters may not recognize (e.g., "if I lose an election doing what I think is right, then so be it," "I did not go into politics to win elections, but to make this country a better place"). On more implicit levels, politicians may reveal their (in)sensitivity to sanction by (not) changing course on a matter when electoral sanctions loom. For instance, a top executive may decide to propose a popular piece of legislation only months or weeks before the election, revealing their anxiety of electoral defeat. Representation may arise to the extent that citizens value politicians' (in)sensitivity to electoral sanctions.

Our understanding of responsiveness as sanction sensitivity largely follows that of Andrew Rehfeld (2009). But note that it deviates from some common uses of the term in quantitative-empirical work (see also Rehfeld, 2009, pp. 218–220). For instance, many people understand responsiveness as the idea that policy or positions change in response to changes in public opinion. In contrast, Rehfeld's (2009) construction of the concept focuses on the underlying sanction sensitivity of the representative that makes them reconsider and potentially amend policy or positions. Essentially, in our view responsiveness refers to the representative's desire or relative indifference about being re-elected, whereas their behavior regarding substantive representation – defined, to recall, as whether a politician advances citizens' policy preferences – is only one signal from which their responsiveness can sometimes be inferred. For instance, if politicians change their substantive policy positions in the direction of their district's majority opinion closely before a very competitive election, many observers will infer that they do so out of high sensitivity to potential electoral sanctions.

Figure 9 shows an example of responsiveness being contained in a communicative act. It is a quote by German foreign minister Annalena Baerbock that fueled a resignation campaign against Baerbock on social media, and made headlines in some traditional media in September 2022. When speaking at the Forum 2000 Conference in Prague on Germany's support for Ukraine, Baerbock said:

> If I give the promise to people in Ukraine "we stand with you as long as you need us," then I want to deliver – no matter what my German voters think. [...] People will go on the street and say "we cannot pay our energy prices" and I will say "yes, I know, so we help you with social measures." But I don't want to say "okay, then we stop the sanctions against Russia." We will stand with Ukraine and this means the sanctions will stay, also in winter time, even if it gets really tough for politicians [...].

Figure 9 Example of responsiveness dimension in communicative act –
German Foreign Minister Annalena Baerbock speaking about support for
Ukraine at Forum 2000 Conference (2022)

Note: "Annalena Baerbock, German Federal Minister for Foreign Affairs, speaking at
the Ukraine Recovery Conference" by UK Foreign, Commonwealth & Development
Office, used under CC BY 2.0/Cropped from the original, text box has been added by the
authors.

Baerbock here states with great clarity that she will *not* be responsive to what
her voters think on Ukraine. But note that, in this quote, the electoral sanction
aspect of responsiveness remains somewhat implicit. While implying that she
does not care about electoral consequences, Baerbock does not explicitly say
that she does "not care about losing an election."

Very little research on citizens' preferences toward representation focuses on
responsiveness understood as sanction sensitivity. A significant related body of
literature asks citizens whether politicians should follow their constituents' or
their own opinions, but it usually does not link this to the idea that politicians
may follow constituents precisely *to avert electoral sanctions* (e.g., Bowler,
2017; Dassonneville et al., 2021; Rosset et al., 2017). While results are mixed,
most of these studies suggest that, on average, citizens might prefer politicians
who follow their constituents' opinions over those who do not (Barker &
Carman, 2012; Bowler, 2017; Wolak, 2017). Bøggild (2016) is one of the few

studies that isolate the effect of electoral sanction sensitivity with experimental methods, showing that citizens actually *dislike* reelection-seeking politicians. In any case, we expect that *authoritarian-libertarian value orientations* are an important source of individuals' general preference for responsiveness. Authoritarian individuals have high levels of respect for authority, they are obedient, and do not seek voice or participation in politics but entrust it to leaders (Inglehart & Flanagan, 1987). This should make them *more approving* of unresponsive politicians, whom they see as authorities, rather than as their agents; and whom they expect to follow principled commitments, rather than the "mob on the street." In contrast, libertarian individuals strive for independence from authorities, value self-expression, and want to actively participate in politics and have a say over communal matters. They should prefer a representative who is foremost a spokesperson of their constituents, amplifying their views, and being highly sensitive to their demands. Since Western mass publics have been subject to stark value change toward more libertarian orientations during the last decades (e.g., Caughey et al., 2019; Flanagan & Lee, 2003), we also expect that older generations will have a weaker preference for responsiveness compared to younger generations.

3.5 Two Clarifications

Let us close our discussion of our conceptual framework with two clarifications.

Clarification #1: Level(s) of analysis. While we have spent almost the entirety of this section on discussing the communicative act as the supposed nucleus of the study of representation, we want to draw attention to the fact that this does not imply that the best *level of analysis* is always the individual communicative act. On an ontological level, we believe representation *is* constituted by communicative acts and their evaluations. But from an epistemological perspective, it may sometimes be advantageous to analyze at a level where communicative acts are already aggregated. Sometimes we may lack data on the act level but have data on a more aggregated level (e.g., when we do not have citizens' evaluations of single communicative acts but of a politician's speech). Similarly, aggregated data may be easier to collect and allow us to rely on larger, less biased data sets. Hence, while it may often be an excellent choice to analyze individual communicative acts (de Wilde, 2013), other levels of analysis may be justifiable in many cases.

Clarification #2: Multidimensionality. While we discussed each dimension of analysis on its own, we would like to remind readers that communicative acts may contain information on none, one, two, or up to all six dimensions of representation that may be salient to different degrees in different communicative acts. When Joe Biden says he will represent all Americans, no matter whether they voted for him or not, he makes a partisan surrogate and a republican justification claim at the same time. He may then go on to speak about the policies with which he intends to achieve his representational aims or highlight his descriptive background that makes him relate to people – adding more dimensions of representation to his claim. Indeed, which dimension(s) are rendered salient by politicians in their representative practice and which are left out is an important issue for further empirical investigation that our framework foregrounds.

4 Empirical Application: Women's Representation in the UK

How can we study political representation empirically if we adopt an interactive constructivist ontology, and conceptualize representation as a communicative practice as previously discussed? In this section, we present one exemplary study of how representation can be studied using the analytical framework proposed in this Element. In short, our analytical framework has two important implications for empirical research. First, in encourages empiricists to *look beyond substantive and descriptive representation*, considering other dimensions of representation also contained in politicians' communicative acts. Second, it reorients our attention from the actions of representatives to how *representatives' behavior relates to how citizens want to be represented* in the first place. Taken together, this amounts to a significant revision of the conventional empirical research agenda on political representation. What started with an ontological shift eventually results in an amended empirical approach to representation.

Our exemplary study focuses on the representation of *female* voters by *female* MPs in the United Kingdom in the run-up to the 2019 general elections. While recent contributions in representation studies have focused on the representation of specific groups like women, ethnic minorities, immigrants or lower social classes, we believe no strand of literature in the field has been as flourishing and impactful during the last years as women's representation (see e.g., Wängnerud, 2009). Showing how our framework can speak to a core theme in current research helps clarify how it can contribute to widening our scholarly perspectives and gaining new insights. Indeed, we demonstrate here how women's representation in the UK fails on dimensions of analysis that have rarely – if ever – been studied before. While female citizens' wishes of how they want to be represented largely correspond to how MPs represent them on the dimensions of *surrogation, justification*, and *responsiveness*, we find that they diverge on *personalization*. Female MPs do not fulfil women's demand for strong party independence.

Before getting started, however, we stress that our study is *exemplary* in the sense that it is meant to illustrate the potential of our analytical framework. We emphatically do not wish to suggest that the research design, data, or methods we use are the only, let alone best, way of studying representation as a communicative practice. Indeed, representation as conceived in this Element can be studied in a variety of different ways, and we see no need to argue a priori for any limitations as far as data or methods are concerned. What matters, to repeat, is to approach political representation in a different, more relational and communication-centered fashion (see Wolkenstein & Wratil, 2021, pp. 873–874). Similarly, our framework is in no way limited to the study of women's representation or of group-based representation more broadly. It can likewise be applied when studying the representation of other groups (e.g., intersectional groups of lesbian or black women) and the public as a whole, or other aspects of representation (e.g., how practices differ between countries).

4.1 The Limitations of Research on Women's Representation

The inclusion of women in national parliaments is widely seen as an important indicator of the strength of democracy. This has given rise to an extensive literature on the growing numbers and influence of women members of parliament in democracies around the world (e.g., Campbell et al., 2010; Dahlerup, 2017; Krook, 2010; Lawless, 2015; Schwindt-Bayer, 2009; Wängnerud, 2009). In this literature, scholars typically reach for the traditional twofold analytical frame of *descriptive* and *substantive* representation; and it has often been argued that greater descriptive representation of women – that is, increased numbers of women in parliaments – improves women's substantive representation – that is, the impact of their interests on policies. As Mansbridge (2005, p. 622) puts it, "[d]escriptive representation by gender improves substantive outcomes for women in every polity for which we have a measure."

This wisdom has been challenged by some feminist scholars. Both the idea that a "critical mass" (Dahlerup, 2017) of women in legislatures improves substantive policy outcomes for women, and received notions of "women's interests" that can be represented in politics, have been called into question. Concerning the "critical mass" argument, for example, Childs and Krook (2006, p. 522) note that "it is increasingly obvious that there is neither a single nor a universal relationship between the percentage of women elected to political office and the passage of legislation beneficial to women as a group." Even more fundamental is the growing "unease among gender and politics scholars regarding universal definitions of 'women's interests,' a priori assumptions about the nature of 'women' as a group, and tendencies to overlook the perspectives of women in civil society by emphasizing the role of female elected officials" (Celis et al., 2014, p. 154).

Taken together, these two lines of critique suggest that it might be worthwhile to approach women's representation beyond its substantive and descriptive dimensions. If it is true that descriptive representation is an unreliable indicator of substantive outcomes, and one must be cautious with assuming that women have specific group interests to begin with, then it seems fruitful to consider alternative analytical frames. Here, we rely on our six dimensions of analysis and particularly focus on those four that are less prominent in the women's representation literature, namely *surrogation, justification, personalization,* and *responsiveness.* However, as we will see next, substantive and descriptive aspects also feature in our analysis.

4.2 Hypotheses about Women's Representation

In this section, we develop the main hypotheses that we want to test empirically. Focusing on our two core components of representation – (1) *representatives' communicative acts* and (2) *citizens' evaluations of representatives' communicative acts* – our guiding questions are as follows. First, *what do women expect from their representatives in terms of surrogation, justification, personalization, and responsiveness?* And second, *to what extent are these demands reflected in female MPs communicative acts?* Note that these research questions are *descriptive.* We are not concerned with whether women's expectations regarding representation are *causally shaped* by female MPs, or whether female MPs are causally induced by their constituents to adopt certain behaviors. Consequently, our hypotheses are also (non-causal) conjectured relationships (Van Evera, 2016). Though we regularly highlight what we believe to be the causes of certain patterns in the development of our hypotheses, with our research design we cannot test these causal effects, but only the presence of patterns. Importantly, we formulate our hypotheses with an eye to the specific context of the UK's political system, and they are sensitive to key findings in the empirical literature on women's representation.

First, with regard to the dimension of *surrogation,* we begin by noting that the UK's SMD electoral system enables surrogate representation in Mansbridge's sense, that is, representation by a representative from another electoral district, with whom one has no electoral relationship. Thus, constituents in the UK may not expect representation from the MP who had been elected in their constituency, but from some other MP from another constituency. Representation demands toward MPs from other constituencies may for one thing be triggered by ideological differences: the MP in one's electoral district might not be from one's preferred party, so one expects representation from an MP from another district who is from the party one supports. When it comes to women's representation, we argue that descriptive representation (Pitkin, 1967) between constituents and the local MP could "cushion" such demands.

Why might this be so? Generally speaking, the literature on women's representation would lead us to expect that female constituents will have weaker representation demands toward MPs from other constituencies as compared to their local MP *if* their local MP is a woman. On the one hand, female constituents may expect, *ceteris paribus*, that female local MPs are more likely to act in their interest, that is, to deliver substantive policy outcomes for women, as they may share similar priorities and preferences (e.g., Mendelberg et al., 2014; O'Brien & Piscopo, 2019; Wängnerud, 2009).[10] On the other hand, unlike vote choice, representation demands are inconsequential for party political control. Hence, while female constituents may not be compelled by gender to vote for a female representative from a party they do not support (Dolan, 2014), they may nevertheless see a female MP from an opposed party more as their representative than a male MP from the same opposed party (see Celis & Erzeel, 2013).

On the representatives' side of the equation, we expect female MPs to generally emphasize surrogation in their communicative acts, talking more about women in general – and not only about women in their district – than male MPs. This has been demonstrated by several studies that deal with surrogate representation in particular. In a study of US congress, Carroll (2002) finds that female legislators view themselves as surrogate representatives of women in the United States, beyond the boundaries of district lines. Pearson and Dancey (2011, p. 515) show that "congresswomen in both parties are more likely than congressmen to discuss women in their speeches. Thus, speeches provide a venue for congresswomen to voice the 'uncrystallized interests' of women across a range of issues." Similar findings are reported by Reingold (2003) and Walsh (2002). Mansbridge (2003, p. 523) theorizes that it is the descriptive under-representation of women in parliaments that induces female MPs to act as surrogate representatives of women: as she argues, the "sense of surrogate responsibility becomes stronger when the surrogate representative shares experiences with surrogate constituents in a way that a majority of the legislature does not. . . . Feelings of responsibility for constituents outside one's

---

[10] Note that this point can be made without assuming that there exists such a thing as objective women's interests: what matters is that female constituents' expectations as to how they are represented are shaped by the fact that they are inclined to perceive female MPs as "similar" in some relevant sense.

district grow even stronger when the legislature includes few, or disproportionately few, representatives of the group in question."

> **H1a (Surrogation, constituent side):** *Female constituents will raise weaker surrogation demands toward MPs elected in other constituencies if their local MP is a woman.*
>
> **H1b (Surrogation, representative side):** *Female MPs will talk more about women as opposed to their constituency than male MPs.*

Second, with regard to *justification*, we argue that the sex of the MP that female constituents pick as their primary representative will influence what sort of justification they demand. Specifically, female constituents will be more likely to demand *pluralist* justification from their chosen MPs if their MP is a woman than if they are a man. From chosen female representatives they will explicitly demand that they justify their actions by appealing to the good of particular social groups, as a proxy for their advocacy of women's concerns. On the other hand, if their chosen MP is male, female constituents will demand more *republican* justification, meaning that they want their MP to justify their actions by appealing to society as a whole. Our explanation of this hypothesis is simple. It has often been argued that female representatives are more likely to focus on what is typically (and not uncontroversially) called "women's issues" than male representatives (e.g., Campbell et al., 2010; Lawless, 2015, p. 359; Norris & Lovenduski, 1995; Reingold, 2000). In other words, female representatives tend to speak more about women as a group with pluralist, specifically group-related concerns than male MPs. We generally expect female constituents to affirm and embrace this, since it enhances their overall representation in politics. Moreover, we expect the hypothesis to hold across political divides, for, as Celis and Childs (2018, p. 10) note, the tendency of female MPs to talk more about women can also be witnessed among conservative female MPs: they just "adopt a different conceptualization of what constitutes women's interests when they address the same issue as other (left/feminist) women representatives."

> **H2a (Justification, constituent side):** *Female constituents will demand more pluralist justification from their chosen MP if she is a woman.*
>
> **H2b (Justification, representative side):** *Female MPs will engage more in pluralist justification than male MPs.*

Third, with regard to *personalization*, we conceptualize party independence in terms of an MP's (communicative act without speech of) voting against their party in the House of Commons. Parliamentary voting is one of the most important tasks of elected representatives, and rebellion against the party whip has accordingly received significant scholarly attention (e.g., Carey, 2007; Slapin et al., 2018). We argue that female constituents will demand *more* personalization from their chosen MP *if* that MP is a woman. The reason is that women are cross-nationally underrepresented in parliaments in general, and in political leadership positions in particular (e.g., Blumenau, 2021; Krook & O'Brien, 2012; Teele et al., 2018; Thomsen & King, 2020). The UK House of Commons is no exception to this rule. Male MPs outnumber female MPs; the leaders of the two major parties are men; and women hold significantly fewer cabinet posts in government, as well as fewer committee chair positions and select committee chairs, relative to their male counterparts (House of Commons Library, 2021, pp. 9–10). Given these widely known gender disparities, female constituents may reasonably expect female MPs to have less influence on parties' parliamentary votes than male MPs. If they then chose a woman as their main representative, they are likely to want that person to be more independent of their party to increase the voice of women within the party. As far as female MPs are concerned, we expect them to generally rebel more often against the party line than male MPs. This, too, is because of women's systematic underrepresentation in key positions: to advance their agenda, they will sometimes have to vote against their party (Barnes, 2016; Papavero & Zucchini, 2018; Wojcik & Mullenax, 2017).

> **H3a (Personalization, constituent side):** *Female constituents will demand more party independence from their chosen MP if she is a woman.*
>
> **H3b (Personalization, representative side):** *Female MPs will rebel more often against the party line than male MPs.*

Finally, the dimension of *responsiveness* refers to MPs' sensitivity to possible electoral sanctions. Note that constituents may demand sanction sensitivity not just from representatives they have an electoral relationship with. They can plausibly hold views about how much sanction sensitivity a given representative should exhibit without being themselves able to elect or unseat that representative, as in the case of surrogate representatives. When it comes to female constituents, we expect them to demand less sanction sensitivity from their chosen MP if that MP is a woman. This expectation is consistent with what we have argued thus far: to the extent that women expect to be better represented by other women than by men (see Mendelberg et al., 2014; O'Brien & Piscopo, 2019; Wängnerud, 2009), they have less reason to want female MPs to be sanction-sensitive than male MPs. On the representatives' side, we hypothesize that female MPs will, on average, be less sanction-sensitive than male MPs. This is because female MPs more often act as advocates for more specific (minority) issues and concerns than their male colleagues, which likely requires resisting swings in majority public opinion (e.g., Campbell et al., 2010; Norris & Lovenduski, 1995).

H4a **(Responsiveness, constituent side):** *Female constituents will demand less sanction sensitivity from their chosen MP if she is a woman.*

H4b **(Responsiveness, representative side):** *Female MPs will be less responsive to public opinion than male MPs.*

4.3 Case and Data

We test our hypotheses in the context of the 2019 UK general election. The 2019 election was characterized by a fierce campaign between the Conservatives and Labour over Brexit, including such divisive issues as whether a second referendum should be held on the country's EU membership. Testing our hypotheses in the context of an election campaign has the advantage of citizens being more aware of MPs due to the salience of the upcoming vote, which should lead to a higher availability of relevant attitudes. While this may impact our results, election campaigns are key periods in which constituents identify with and relate to representatives, and representatives directly engage with constituents. Hence, they are particularly relevant for the constitution of representative relationships. To test our hypotheses on the constituent as well as the representative side, we use existing data from publicly available sources on MPs' behavior as well as an original survey on representation preferences of the general adult UK population. We conducted this survey on the online survey platform *Prolific Academic* between 26 and 28 November 2019, at the peak of the campaign, two weeks ahead of the 12 December election. Using Prolific's stratified sampling, our sample ($n = 1,310$) is representative of the UK general (18+ age) population for age, sex and ethnicity, but all our results draw on female respondents only ($n = 671$).

4.3.1 Measures on the Constituents' Side

We use our survey to operationalize citizens' preferences on all four dimensions of representation. First, for citizens' demands for surrogation we present our respondents with a set of different MPs to report to what extent they see each as a political representative of themselves. Specifically, we survey opinion toward (1) their local MP (elected in the 2017 UK general election in their constituency), (2) the party leaders of all four major UK parties (Conservative, Labour, Liberal Democrat, Scottish National Party), and (3) one random MP (drawn from all remaining 649 constituencies). The specific question wording is: "How much do you consider each of the following individuals someone who speaks and acts for you in politics?" Respondents rate each MP, introduced with his/her name plus constituency (e.g., "Jeremy Corbyn (MP for Islington North)"), on a scale from "1 – Not at all" to "7 – Very much." We operationalize demand for surrogation as the maximum scale value given by a respondent for any of the MPs that were *not* elected in her constituency minus the value given to the local MP (with a range from –6 to 6, with higher values indicating demand for surrogation). Hence, territorial surrogation demands are stronger if a respondent strongly views, for instance, a national party leader as her representative but not at all her local MP – and vice versa.

In addition, we also ask respondents to actually choose one of the listed MPs as their primary representative ("And which of these individuals do you consider the person who speaks and acts for you most in politics?"). This operationalizes the concept of the "chosen MP" we use in the theory section, and it allows us to let respondents assess the remaining three dimensions of representation about their chosen MP. For the justification dimension we ask: "When *Name of chosen MP* speaks about policies, do you want her/him to refer more to people like you or to society as a whole?" The scale ranges from "1 – People like me" to "7 – Society as a whole," capturing respondents' demands for more republican versus pluralist justification. Here, "people like me" simply represents one alternative among many for pluralist justifications (e.g., "people in my constituency," "the poor"), which we viewed as particularly salient and easy to understand for respondents, but projects could investigate demands for various forms of pluralist justification. For the personalization dimension, our question is: "How much do you want *Name of chosen MP* to speak and act independently of her/his party?" The scale values range from "1 – Very little" to "7 – A lot." While our question aims at a generic, encompassing understanding of personalization, researchers could also investigate attitudes toward specific aspects of personalization (e.g., independent campaigning, voting in rebellion to the party, performing tasks for the party machinery).

Last, we operationalize demands for responsiveness with the following question: "Politicians' own convictions are sometimes in conflict with what voters want. In such situations, they can follow their convictions at the cost of losing votes in the next election, or do what voters want to win or retain votes. What do you want *Name of chosen MP* to do in such situations?" The six answer categories range from "Always follow own convictions" to "Always follow voters," with degrees indicated by "Primarily follow ... " and "Rather follow ... " and no middle category. While we pit sanction sensitivity against politicians' own convictions, other projects could operationalize alternative opposites to sanction sensitivity. Hence, our justification measure runs from 1 to 7 (higher values indicating demand for republican aims), our personalization measure from 1 to 7 (higher values indicating more demand for independence from the party), and our responsiveness measure from 1 to 6 (higher values indicating more demand for sanction sensitivity).

In addition to these questions, we also asked respondents about various covariates (see the Online Appendix for details). In all models on the constituent side, we control for respondents' left-right self-placement and vote intention in a potential second Brexit referendum, as ideology may influence representation preferences but may also affect whether women choose a female MP as their representative. We also control for the party that respondents feel closest to as partisanship may impact on women's representation preferences but may also shape whether women view a female MP as their representative. Last, we control for whether the respondent has a university degree (dummy variable) as well as their age, as these are key determinants of representation preferences but could also influence whether women's chosen MP is female (e.g., different views on emancipation in different cohorts or education strata).

4.3.2 Measures on the Representatives' Side

We draw on House of Commons speech and divisions data for the 2017–2019 Parliament to operationalize MPs' communicative acts on the four dimensions of representation. Our speech data comprises all floor speeches and interventions in the House of Commons, which were obtained from www.theyworkfor you.com. Our divisions data comprises all divisions in the House of Commons and was obtained from www.publicwhiporg.uk.

First, to measure the extent to which MPs engage in surrogate representation for women, we measure how often they speak about females as a group living across the country as opposed to their local constituency in their speeches. To count references to women, we draw on the Linguistic Inquiry and Word Count (LIWC) dictionary that contains a category for women, consisting of words such as "girl," "lady," "madam" but also pronouns like "she" and "her" (see Pennebaker et al., 2015). For constituency references, we count the number of mentions of the constituency's name as well as the use of the words "constituency" and "constituents" (see Kellermann, 2015; McKay, 2020). In each case, we use the percentage of women/constituency references as of all words spoken by the MP. Our measure of surrogation then is the z-score standardized percentage of women references minus the z-standardized percentage of constituency references. Importantly, the LIWC women category has been used as a measure of women's representation in various projects (e.g., Pearson & Dancey, 2011).

Second, we measure justification styles from MPs' speeches, by drawing on a combination of dictionaries with a locally trained word-embedding model (see Rodriguez & Spirling, 2022). Our approach closely follows that by Hargrave and Blumenau (2022) who pioneered the use of word-embeddings to improve standard dictionaries of political rhetorical styles, also focusing on speech in the House of Commons. In a first step, we define two "seed dictionaries" that contain words that we deem representative of pluralist and republican justification styles, respectively. Whereas the pluralist seed dictionary includes references to groups such as "employees," "disadvantaged," "businesswomen," or "veterans," the republican dictionary includes words that signal an appeal to the whole of society such as "society," "taxpayers," "United Kingdom," "everyone," or "collectively." The word embeddings model allows us to refine these seed dictionaries. It identifies words in parliamentary speeches with a similar semantic meaning to the average word in each seed dictionary, that is, words that should be included in the dictionaries. But it also allows us to eliminate words from the seed dictionaries whose semantic meaning is far off from other words in the dictionary. Based on a validation exercise, our final measure captures the use of pluralist justification styles only and has a theoretical range from 0 to 1, with higher values indicating that an MP speaks more republican in the House of Commons. Details are in the Online Appendix.

Third, we measure MPs' personalization from their party based on their rebellion against the party whip in divisions in the House of Commons. Voting represents one of the clearest and most salient acts of rebellion that has been studied widely (e.g., Kam, 2009; Slapin et al., 2018). The fact that party unity in roll-call votes in the House of Commons is rather high and strongly enforced through threats of sanctions (Kam, 2009) renders defections from the party line in voting a particularly strong signal of party independence of an MP. Specifically, we rely on the MPs' rate of rebellion as the percentage of all votes in the House of Commons on which the MP voted against the majority of her party's MPs during the 2017–2019 session.

Fourth, we build a measure of responsiveness as the MP's sanction sensitivity. This is the most challenging task as MPs' sensitivity to electoral sanctions is not directly observable but must be inferred from whether and how they potentially change their behavior in response to a change in the expectation of electoral sanctions. In other words, it must be inferred from observable implications. We exploit the fact that the issue of Brexit was central to not only the period from 2017 to 2019 but also to the election campaign. The Conservative Party campaigned on the slogan "Get Brexit Done," and the issue always figured at the top of concerns in opinion polls (see Prescott-Smith, 2019). Hence, MPs could expect electoral sanctions from not responding to their constituents on this issue. Moreover, the fact that the 2019 election was a snap election highlights that many MPs might not have expected to face an electoral race at the end of the year. Indeed, Labour had for a long time refused to agree to the 12 December 2019 election (Proctor, 2019). We exploit these circumstances and investigate how MPs shifted their positions on Brexit between the first months of 2019 and the period after Boris Johnson had become prime minister. As it had been known that Johnson was keen to call a snap election (Mattinson, 2019), MPs should have increased their expectations of a future electoral contest after the 2019 summer recess of the House of Commons. Essentially, we exploit an increase in the imminence of electoral sanctions to observe which MPs are reacting to it to what extent and therefore are more/less sensitive to sanctions.

In a first step, we estimate MPs' ideal points on Brexit (pro vs. against) before and after Johnson took office/the summer recess using a Bayesian dynamic item-response theory (IRT) model on Brexit-related divisions in the House of Commons. We first identified fifty votes on Brexit issues (e.g., May's meaningful votes, indicative votes, Cooper-Letwin Bill and Benn Act) throughout 2019, of which forty-two fell before and eight after the summer recess. This provides us with two ideal points on Brexit for each MP – one before and one after the summer recess. The details of this model are in the Online Appendix. In a second step, we build our actual measure of responsiveness by conceptually defining "perfect responsiveness" as a change in positions on Brexit between the two periods that is *fully explained by concerns about electoral sanctions*. We argue that MPs who face pro-Brexit public opinion in their constituency should move their ideal point toward Brexit, and those that face anti-Brexit opinion should move it away from Brexit to demonstrate sanction sensitivity to their voters. However, there are some caveats. If an MP holds a constituency by a large vote margin, they effectively face no plausible electoral sanction, as they can expect to defend their seat, no matter how they position themselves on Brexit. Hence, we focus on a subset of those MPs that had a realistic chance to be unseated, which we define as a vote margin of <10 percent to the runner-up in the 2017 general election. We exclude all other, "safe" MPs from the analysis. Moreover, MPs that already were quite pro-Brexit or anti-Brexit in period one, have less need to move their ideal points further. In sum, we set up an OLS model with the position change on Brexit as the dependent variable and the percentage of the Brexit vote in the MP's constituency in the 2016 referendum (taken from Hanretty, 2017) as well as the MP's position before the summer recess as covariates. This is a model of "perfect responsiveness." Consequently, we can use the (absolute) residuals of this model as our measure of MPs' lack of responsiveness. The intuition behind this is: the less we can explain the MP's position change on Brexit by electoral factors in our model, the less responsive to electoral sanctions the MP is.

In addition to these main measures, we also use three control variables on the representative side in most models. We control for MPs' party affiliation with a categorical variable, which accounts for the fact that parties may influence representation on the different dimensions (e.g., on personalization) and that the number of female MPs also varies by party. We also control for MP's position on a left-right dimension, as the ideological position of an MP may shape their behavior on different dimensions of representation and female MPs are known to be more leftist than male MPs, on average (see the Online Appendix for how this measure is constructed). As a third control variable for the representative side, we include the percentage of the Brexit vote in the MP's constituency in the 2016 referendum (taken from Hanretty, 2017), as constituents' Brexit preferences may influence MPs' behavior on multiple dimensions (e.g., justification, personalization). We only omit this for the responsiveness model, as the variable is part of the measurement of MPs' responsiveness.

In all our models, we also include the unemployment rate (%) on 1 November 2019 (provided by the House of Commons Library) in either the MP's constituency (on the representative side) or the local/chosen MP's constituency (on the constituent side). We view unemployment as a key proxy for the socioeconomic situation of a constituency that may not only influence MPs' representation practice but also what exactly constituents demand from their local or chosen representative (e.g., they may adjust their personal demands due to sociotropic concerns).

4.4 Analysis and Results

All our models are linear regression models with clustered standard errors for different sets of MPs on the constituent side and nonclustered standard errors on the representative side. While on the constituent side we only draw on our sample of female voters, on the representative side we draw on all MPs for which we have full data in each model.

4.4.1 Analyses on the Constituent Side

All results for the constituent side are reported in Table 3. They show the estimates for key variables. Full results with all covariates are in the Online Appendix. To test hypothesis H1a whether women raise weaker surrogation demands toward MPs outside their constituency if their local MP is a woman, we regress our respondents' surrogation demand on a binary indicator for their local MP being female. We also include our standard set of controls (in this case, including the unemployment rate in the local MP's/the respondent's constituency). Moreover, since the demand for surrogation should be strongly

Table 3 Regression models on the constituent side

	Model 1a	Model 2a	Model 3a	Model 4a
	Surrogation	**Justification**	**Personalization**	**Responsiveness**
Female local MP	−0.678			
	(0.205)**			
Female chosen MP		−0.386	0.417	−0.006
		(0.165)*	(0.170)*	(0.118)
N	671	671	659	669
Standard controls	Included	Included	Included	Included
Additional controls	Copartisan, local MP standing down	Chosen MP	Party of chosen MP	Chosen MP standing down
Clustering of standard errors	Local MP	Chosen MP	Chosen MP	Chosen MP

Note: All are linear regression models; Clustered standard errors in parentheses; * *p<0.05*; ** *p<0.01*.

influenced by whether the local MP is from the party a respondent feels closest to, we include a dummy variable indicating such situations. This is important to rule out that the effects of descriptive representation do not only reflect a correlation of the share of women MPs in parties and the share of female supporters of parties. Last, we include a dummy for whether the local MP stood down in the 2019 election, as this may incentivize respondents to demand more surrogation. Model 1a in Table 3 shows that if the respondent's local MP is also female, demands for surrogation are significantly weaker. This effect is statistically significant at the 1 percent level and fully in line with hypothesis H1a. *Descriptive representation in the constituency significantly diminishes women's demand for representation by other politicians.* We plot women's surrogation demand depending on whether their local MP is a woman in the upper left panel of Figure 10. The magnitude of the effect is very substantial at around half a standard deviation of the dependent variable.

Next, we test hypothesis H2 that women will demand more pluralist justification from their chosen MP if she is female. We regress respondents' demand for republican justification on a dummy variable for whether the chosen MP is female. We also include our standard set of controls (including the unemployment rate in the chosen MP's constituency; the same in the following models). The results are reported as Model 2a and provide significant support for the hypothesis. *Women who choose female MPs as their representative demand significantly less republican but more pluralist justification from them than women who choose a male MP.* This suggests that women who identify women as their representatives expect them to represent women's pluralist group interests. The effect is plotted in the upper-left panel of Figure 10 and represents a change of about 0.23 standard deviations in constituents' justification demands.

To test hypothesis H3a that female constituents will demand more party independence if their chosen MP is a woman as opposed to a man, we again draw on the binary indicator for the chosen MP being female. In addition to our standard controls, we also control for the party affiliation of the chosen MP, since constituents may consider to what extent rebellion is tolerated in each party when forming their personalization demands. Again, we find clear support for our hypothesis as reported in Model 3a, suggesting that *women who view female MPs as their representatives want them to increase the voice for women and their issues within the party.* The effect plotted in the lower left panel of Figure 10 is about 0.26 standard deviations in the dependent variable.

Finally, we test H4a – whether women demand less responsiveness from female MPs than from male MPs. Besides our standard set of controls, we also again control with a dummy for chosen MPs that stood down in the 2019 election, as women who identify with such MPs may demand significantly

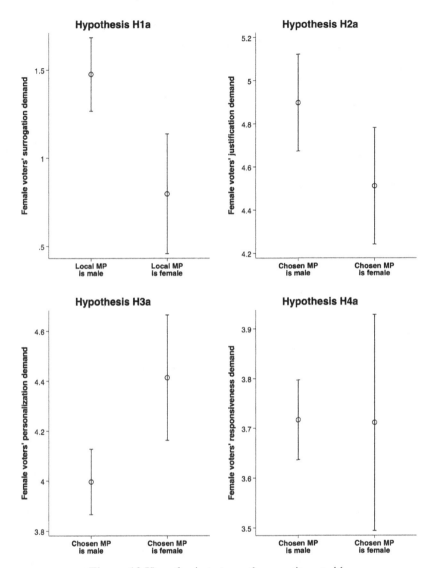

Figure 10 Hypothesis tests on the constituent side
Note: Estimates from linear regression models; 95 percent confidence intervals as vertical lines.

less responsiveness from them. The insignificant coefficient on the dummy for female chosen MPs in Model 4a suggests that *female constituents' responsiveness demands are the same toward male and female MPs*. Hence, we do not find any support for H4a. Women have no special expectations toward female MPs in terms of how sensitive they should be to electoral defeat. We plot this null effect in the lower-right panel of Figure 10.

4.4.2 Analyses on the Representative Side

All results for the representative side are reported in Table 4. They show estimates for the key variables. Full results are in the Online Appendix. To test hypothesis H1b that female MPs engage in more surrogate representation for women by talking about them in Parliament, we regress the focus on women references as opposed to constituency references on a dummy for female MPs as well as our standard controls. The results in Model 1b show that female MPs indeed speak significantly more about women compared to their constituency than male MPs. The effect is 0.60 standard deviations – a very substantial effect by any standard. We plot this effect in the upper-left panel of Figure 11. Women MPs therefore follow female constituents' demands for surrogate representation (see discussion earlier). Our analyses therefore reveal some *substantial correspondence between female constituents' preferences for representation and female MPs' practices of representation on the surrogation dimension.*

To test hypothesis H2b that female MPs will engage in more pluralist as opposed to republican justification than male MPs, we regress MPs' justification style from our word embeddings model on the female MP dummy and our standard controls. Again, the results in Model 2b yield clear support for our hypothesis. Female MPs score about 0.61 standard deviations lower on the republican vs. pluralist justification score than male MPs. This is a very substantial effect that we plot in the upper-right panel of Figure 11. It suggests that *female MPs represent women's preferences for pluralist justification in their parliamentary work, resulting in substantial correspondence on this dimension of representation.*

Next, we test hypothesis H3b that female MPs will be more party independent than their male counterparts by regressing MPs' rate of rebellion on the female MP dummy as well as our standard controls. Note that we exclude MPs that had no political party affiliation at the end of the legislative term, as we lack rates of rebellion for them. The results in Model 3b provide no support for our hypothesis. Female MPs are neither more nor less rebellious in the House of Commons. This is illustrated in the lower-left panel of Figure 11 by the wide overlap of the confidence intervals. It suggests that *female representatives do not act in line with female constituents' preferences for higher personalization, at least not in the communicative act of voting against the party line.* Our results thereby reveal some deficits in representation on this dimension.

Last, we test whether female MPs engage in less responsiveness than male MPs (hypothesis H4b). For this purpose, we regress our measure of irresponsiveness on the female MP dummy and our standard set of controls. Model 4b provides *no evidence for a statistically significant effect of the MP's gender.* The

Table 4 Regression models on the representative side

	Model 1b	Model 2b	Model 3b	Model 4b
	Surrogation	**Justification**	**Personalization**	**Responsiveness**
Female MP	0.603	0.019	−0.144	0.002
	(0.121)**	(0.002)**	(0.256)	(0.035)
N	628	628	585	159
Standard controls	Included	Included	Included	Included, except for Brexit vote

Note: All are linear regression models; Standard errors in parentheses; * *p*<0.05; ** *p*<0.01.

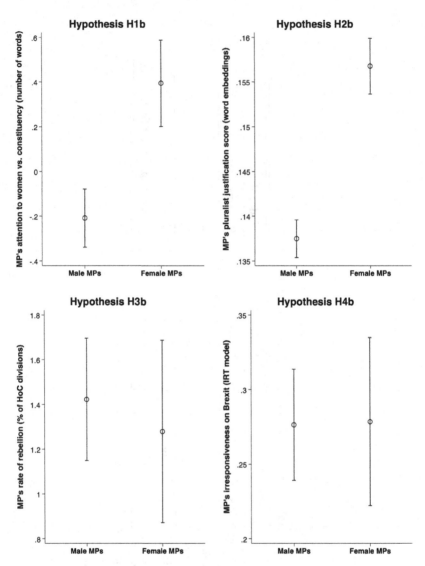

Figure 11 Hypothesis tests on the representative side

Note: Estimates from linear regression models; 95 percent confidence intervals as vertical lines.

coefficient on the female MP dummy is indistinguishable from zero. But this equal level of responsiveness of male and female MPs is in line with female constituents' demands for the same responsiveness from both genders (see discussion earlier). Hence, *female constituents' preferences and MPs' actions on the responsiveness dimension are actually in correspondence with each other.*

4.5 Making Sense of the Findings

Let us summarize our findings. The high levels of correspondence between voters' wishes and MPs' behavior on the *surrogation* and *justification* dimensions confirm our theoretical expectations: the fact that female MPs speak more about women and hence meet the surrogation demands of female voters, in particular of women whose constituency MP is male, and the fact that female MPs generally seem to meet women's demands for pluralist justification in their parliamentary work – all of this is squarely in line with what feminist and women's representation scholars typically anticipate. On the *responsiveness* dimension, our theoretical expectations of female voters wanting less sanction-sensitive MPs and female MPs eyeing less at the next elections found no support. However, the equal level of responsiveness of female and male MPs is reflected in women's expectations toward MPs. In contrast, on the dimension of *personalization*, we found that women want female MPs to increase the voice for women and their issues within the party, but this does not translate into high levels of personalization qua female MPs voting against the party line.

Normatively, the most straightforward conclusion to take from all of this is that surrogation, justification, and responsiveness are three dimensions of women's representation where representation "works well," while the quality of representation is lower on the dimension of personalization. Note, however, that we measure constituents' preferences and MPs' behavior on different scales here (e.g., survey scales vs. measures from text/voting models). Therefore, we can ascertain whether patterns on each side correspond, but cannot directly determine whether the *level* of MPs behavior (e.g., sanction sensitivity) exactly matches citizens' wishes. Moreover, recall that we are only comparing female citizens' *general preferences toward representation* with female MPs' communicative activities here. We are not analyzing the *actual evaluations of female MPs' communicative acts by citizens*. We expect that, if MPs' behavior meets citizens' broad preferences of how they want to be represented, this will be reflected in citizens' evaluations of representation – and their positive evaluations of representatives' actions will in turn bestow legitimacy on representation. But ultimately, we cannot take a conclusive position on whether this is the case with female voters and their representatives in the UK based on this research design.

This is no doubt a limitation of our exemplary study. Yet the point and purpose of that study was not to demonstrate how all things that matter theoretically can be studied empirically. Nor do we think that each and every study that employs our framework must try to operationalize our framework in its entirety. What matters most, we think, is to devise and experiment with empirical research designs that treat representation as a relational and multidimensional phenomenon at the heart of which are communicative acts by representatives. Looking at four out of six dimensions of analyses, a set of nonexhaustive communicative activities by MPs across dimensions, and citizens' preferences rather than evaluations regarding each dimension, our study of women's representation in the UK is but one example of how this can be done. We hope that our theoretical toolkit will inspire quantitative researchers to try out alternative ways of studying representation as a communicative practice.

5 Conclusion

Although the present Element is rather short, the argument we have developed has taken us over a wide terrain:

- In the Introduction, we have drawn attention to the fact that while political scientists have declared a "crisis of representation," public opinion data shows no clear cross-country decline in how citizens' evaluate representation. From our perspective, this calls for resetting our research agenda on the topic.
- In Section 2, we have done some essential theoretical groundwork and proposed an ontological shift toward a relational and communication-centered ontology of representation, which we call *interactive constructivism*.
- In Section 3, we have distinguished two core components of a relational and communication-centered understanding of representation, namely, (a) *representatives' communicative acts* and (b) *citizens' evaluations of representatives' communicative acts*, and then have gone on to examine what representatives may convey in their communicative acts as well as what kinds of attitudes and identities may shape citizens' evaluations of such acts.
- Finally, in Section 4, we have demonstrated how the analytical framework developed in Section 3 may be translated into empirical research designs, and presented an exemplary study of women's representation in the UK that makes use of standard quantitative methods used widely in the field.

What is crucial for us and deserving of renewed emphasis is that we think of our theoretical framework as an *enabling*, rather than constraining, framework. It does not commit researchers to studying only a particular set of dimensions of representation, or to studying all of the six suggested dimensions (i.e., substantive representation, descriptive representation, surrogation, justification, personalization, and responsiveness) at the same time. Nor do we see any principled reason against expanding the set of dimensions that may matter to citizens beyond the six dimensions that we discussed. If scholars were to develop new dimensions of representation building on our framework in the future, we would take this to be a welcome contribution. Nor, again, do we want to suggest that representation as a communicative practice can only be studied using specific research designs, a specific palette of methods, or a specific causal model. Our conceptual framework can be used for a variety of research designs and methods, and interactive constructivism is open to different causal models of how representatives and constituents relate to and influence each other. Moreover, although our primary audience were quantitative scholars, we think that our framework can equally usefully be employed by qualitative researchers – not least to investigate unelected forms of representation that, as we explained in the beginning of Section 3, cannot easily be studied with quantitative methods. In short, this Element offers a novel conceptual toolbox for studying representation that can be used in a variety of different ways and for a range of different intellectual purposes. The only thing that one needs to commit to when employing our conceptual tools is an interactive constructivist ontology of representation. This is, so to speak, a *philosophical* prerequisite and the key to consistency in choosing research strategies and interpreting findings.

Even sympathetic empiricists who read this Element might still wonder whether we got our priorities wrong. Why put so much efforts and energies into theorizing about political representation and addressing meta issues like representation's ontology, when one could instead devise better *methods* for studying representation? The answer is that *ontology is logically prior to epistemology and methodology*, as argued in Section 2. And, to be sure, the impasse that empirical research on representation has reached is certainly not the result of a lack of sophisticated research methods. It is, in our reading, a product of insufficient theoretical reflection about what it is that we are studying when we are studying political representation. One symptom of this is the excessive focus in empirical scholarship on the elusive notion of substantive representation qua responsiveness, a theoretical frame that – contrary to popular belief – even Hanna Pitkin (1967, p. 233) cast doubt on when she suggested that responsiveness may be satisfied when citizens are "unaware of what [the government] is doing," which may be the case "most of the time" (on this point, also see Disch, 2021, pp. 35–39). Another symptom is empirical scholars' near-total neglect of the innovative new theoretical literature on political representation (see Wolkenstein & Wratil, 2021, pp. 864–865). In this Element, we have sought to overcome both of these limitations, closely engaging with the emerging theoretical literature on political representation and moving beyond a focus on the single dimension of substantive representation. We do not claim that our solution of conceiving representation relationally, multidimensionally, and as based on communicative acts is faultless or that we can resolve all theoretical problems with political representation more broadly (note that established approaches to studying representation cannot satisfy this desideratum either, see Sabl, 2015). Nonetheless, we think and hope that our suggested approach can serve as a starting point for debate and new directions for the field. We are hopeful, that is, that scholars will receive from this Element useful impulses for studying political representation in new ways.

References

Achen, C., & Bartels, L. (2017). *Democracy for Realists: Why Elections Do Not Produce Responsive Government*. Princeton University Press.

Amsalem, E., & Zoizner, A. (2020). Real, but Limited: A Meta-Analytic Assessment of Framing Effects in the Political Domain. *British Journal of Political Science*, *52*(1), 221–237.

Arnesen, S., Duell, D., & Johannesson, M. P. (2019). Do Citizens Make Inferences from Political Candidate Characteristics when Aiming for Substantive Representation? *Electoral Studies*, *57*, 46–60.t

Austin, J. L. (1975). *How to Do Things with Words*, 2nd Edition, J. O. Urmson, & M. Sbisà (Eds.). Cambridge.

Barker, D. C., & Carman, C. J. (2012). How Do We Want to Be Represented? How Do We Differ? In *Representing Red and Blue: How the Culture Wars Change the Way Citizens Speak and Politicians Listen, 1st Edition* (pp. 21–38). Oxford University Press.

Barnes, T. D. (2016). *Gendering Legislative Behavior: Institutional Constraints and Collaborations*. Cambridge University Press.

Bartels, L. M. (2002). Beyond the Running Tally: Partisan Bias in Political Perceptions. *Political Behavior*, *24*(2), 117–150.

Bevir, M. (2008). Meta-Methodology: Clearing the Underbrush. In Janet M. Box-Steffensmeier, H. E. Brady, & D. Collier (Eds.), *The Oxford Handbook of Political Methodology* (pp. 48–70). Oxford University Press.

Bevir, M., & Blakely, J. (2015). Naturalism and Anti-naturalism. In M. Bevir, & R. A. W. Rhodes (Eds.), *Routledge Handbook of Interpretive Political Science* (pp. 31–44). Routledge.

Bevir, M., & Kedar, A. (2008). Concept Formation in Political Science: An Anti-naturalist Critique of Qualitative Methodology. *Perspectives on Politics*, *6*(3), 503–517.

Bisgaard, M., & Slothuus, R. (2018). Partisan Elites as Culprits? How Party Cues Shape Partisan Perceptual Gaps. *American Journal of Political Science*, *62*(2), 456–469.

Blumenau, J. (2021). The Effects of Female Leadership on Women's Voice in Political Debate. *British Journal of Political Science*, *51*(2), 750–771.

Bøggild, T. (2016). How Politicians' Reelection Efforts Can Reduce Public Trust, Electoral Support, and Policy Approval. *Political Psychology*, *37*(6), 901–919.

Bøggild, T. (2020). Politicians as Party Hacks: Party Loyalty and Public Distrust in Politicians. *Journal of Politics*, *82*(4), 1517–1529.

Bøggild, T., & Pedersen, H. H. (2020). Voter Reaction to Legislator Dissent across Political Systems. *Electoral Studies*, *68*, 1–7.

Bowler, S. (2017). Trustees, Delegates, and Responsiveness in Comparative Perspective. *Comparative Political Studies*, *50*(6), 766–793.

Bullock, J. G. (2011). Elite Influence on Public Opinion in an Informed Electorate. *American Political Science Review*, *105*(3), 496–515.

Campbell, R., Childs, S., & Lovenduski, J. (2010). Do Women Need Women Representatives? *British Journal of Political Science*, *40*(1), 171–194.

Campbell, R., Cowley, P., Vivyan, N., & Wagner, M. (2019). Legislator Dissent as a Valence Signal. *British Journal of Political Science*, *49*(1), 105–128.

Carey, J. M. (2007). Competing Principals, Political Institutions, and Party Unity in Legislative Voting. *American Journal of Political Science*, *51*(1), 92–107.

Carmines, E. G., & Stimson, J. A. (1980). The Two Faces of Issue Voting. *American Political Science Review*, *74*(1), 78–91.

Caroll, S. (2002). Representing Women: Congresswomen's Perceptions of Their Representational Roles, Oklahoma.

Castanho Silva, B., & Wratil, C. (2023). Do Parties' Representation Failures Affect Populist Attitudes? Evidence from a Multinational Survey Experiment. *Political Science Research and Methods*, *11*(2), 347–362.

Caughey, D., O'Grady, T., & Warshaw, C. (2019). Policy Ideology in European Mass Publics, 1981–2016. *American Political Science Review*, *113*(3), 674–693.

Celis, K., & Childs, S. (2018). Conservatism and Women's Political Representation. *Politics & Gender*, *14*(1), 5–26.

Celis, K., Childs, S., Kantola, J., & Krook, M. L. (2014). Constituting Women's Interests through Representative Claims. *Politics & Gender*, *10*(2), 149–174.

Celis, K., & Erzeel, S. (2013). Gender and Ethnicity: Intersectionality and the Politics of Group Representation in the Low Countries. *Representation*, *49*(4), 487–499.

Childs, S., & Krook, M. L. (2006). Should Feminists Give Up on Critical Mass? A Contingent Yes. *Politics & Gender*, *2*(4), 522–530.

Converse, P. E. (1964). The Nature of Belief Systems in Mass Publics. In D. E. Apter (Ed.), *Ideology and Discontent* (pp. 206–261). The Free Press.

Costa, M. (2020). Ideology, Not Affect: What Americans Want from Political Representation. *American Journal of Political Science*, *65*(2), 342–358.

Dahlberg, S., Linde, J., & Holmberg, S. (2014). Democratic Discontent in Old and New Democracies: Assessing the Importance of Democratic Input and Governmental Output. *Political Studies*, *63*(1), 18–37.

Dahlerup, D. (2017). *Has Democracy Failed Women?* John Wiley & Sons.

Dassonneville, R., Blais, A., Sevi, S., & Daoust, J. F. (2021). How Citizens Want Their Legislator to Vote. *Legislative Studies Quarterly, 46*(2), 297–321.

Dassonneville, R., & McAllister, I. (2018). Gender, Political Knowledge, and Descriptive Representation: The Impact of Long-Term Socialization. *American Journal of Political Science, 62*(2), 249–265.

de Jong, J. C., & Mügge, L. (2023). Super Politicians? Perspectives of Minoritized Citizens on Representation. *Political Studies Review, 21*(3), 506–514.

de Wilde, P. (2013). Representative Claims Analysis: Theory Meets Method. *Journal of European Public Policy, 20*(2), 278–294.

Disch, L. (2011). Toward a Mobilization Conception of Democratic Representation. *American Political Science Review, 105*(1), 100–114.

Disch, L. (2015). The "Constructivist Turn" in Democratic Representation: A Normative Dead-End? *Constellations, 22*(4), 487–499.

Disch, L. (2019). Introduction: The End of Representative Politics. In L. Disch, M. van de Sande, & N. Urbinati (Eds.), *The Constructivist Turn in Political Representation* (pp. 1–18). Edinburgh University Press.

Disch, L. J. (2021). *Making Constituencies: Representation as Mobilization in Mass Democracy.* University of Chicago Press.

Dolan, K. (2014). *When Does Gender Matter?: Women Candidates and Gender Stereotypes in American Elections.* Oxford University Press.

Downs, A. (1957). *An Economic Theory of Democracy.* Harper & Row.

Druckman, J. N. (2004). Political Preference Formation: Competition, Deliberation, and the (Ir)relevance of Framing Effects. *American Political Science Review, 98*(4), 671–686.

Druckman, J. N., Peterson, E., & Slothuus, R. (2013). How Elite Partisan Polarization Affects Public Opinion Formation. *American Political Science Review, 107*(1), 57–79.

Duell, D., Kaftan, L., Proksch, S.-O., Slapin, J., & Wratil, C. (2023). Communicating the Rift: Voter Perceptions of Intraparty Dissent in Parliaments. *The Journal of Politics, 85*(1), 76–91.

Duell, D., Kaftan, L., Proksch, S.-O., Slapin, J., & Wratil, C. (2024). The Rhyme and Reason of Rebel Support: Exploring European Voters' Attitudes toward Dissident MPs. *Political Science Research and Methods, 12*, 301–317.

Easton, D. (2009). A Re-assessment of the Concept of Political Support. *British Journal of Political Science, 5*(4), 435–457.

Ezrow, L., & Xezonakis, G. (2011). Citizen Satisfaction with Democracy and Parties' Policy Offerings. *Comparative Political Studies, 44*(9), 1152–1178.

Fearon, J. D. (1999). Electoral Accountability and the Control of Politicians: Selecting Good Types vs. Sanctioning Poor Performance. In A. Przeworski,

S. C. Stokes, & B. Manin (Eds.), *Democracy, Accountability, and Representation* (pp. 55–97). Cambridge University Press.

Ferrín, M., & Kriesi, H. (2016). *How Europeans View and Evaluate Democracy*. Oxford University Press.

Fiorina, M. P., & Abrams, S. J. (2012). *Disconnect: The Breakdown of Representation in American Politics*. University of Oklahoma Press.

Flanagan, S. C., & Lee, A.-R. (2003). The New Politics, Culture Wars, and the Authoritarian-Libertarian Value Change in Advanced Industrial Democracies. *Comparative Political Studies, 36*(3), 235–270.

Fossen, T. (2019). Constructivism and the Logic of Political Representation. *American Political Science Review, 113*(3), 824–837.

Geenens, R. (2019). Political Representation: The View from France. In L. Disch, M. van de Sande, & N. Urbinati (Eds.), *The Constructivist Turn in Political Representation* (pp. 89–103). Edinburgh University Press.

Geer, J. G. (1996). *From Tea Leaves to Opinion Polls: A Theory of Democratic Leadership*. Columbia University Press.

Gilens, M. (2012). *Affluence and Influence: Economic Inequality and Political Power in America*. Princeton University Press.

Green, J. E. (2010). *The Eyes of the People: Democracy in an Age of Spectatorship*. Oxford University Press.

Greene, Z. D., & Haber, M. (2015). The Consequences of Appearing Divided: An Analysis of Party Evaluations and Vote Choice. *Electoral Studies, 37,* 15–27.

Habermas, J. (1981). *Theorie des kommunikativen Handelns: Band 1. Handlungsrationalität gesellschaftliche Rationalisierung*. Suhrkamp.

Habermas, J. (1998). *Between Facts and Norms: Contributions to a Discourse Theory of Law and Democracy*. MIT Press.

Habermas, J. (2006). Political Communication in Media Society: Does Democracy Still Enjoy an Epistemic Dimension? The Impact of Normative Theory on Empirical Research. *Communication Theory, 16*(4), 411–426.

Halikiopoulou, D., & Vasilopoulou, S. (2016). Breaching the Social Contract: Crises of Democratic Representation and Patterns of Extreme Right Party Support. *Government and Opposition, 53*(1), 26–50.

Hanretty, C. (2017). Areal Interpolation and the UK's Referendum on EU Membership. *Journal of Elections, Public Opinion and Parties, 27*(4), 466–483.

Harden, J. J. (2015). Citizen Demand for the Dimensions of Representation. In *Multidimensional Democracy* (pp. 50–83). Cambridge University Press.

Hargrave, L., & Blumenau, J. (2022). No Longer Conforming to Stereotypes? Gender, Political Style and Parliamentary Debate in the UK. *British Journal of Political Science, 52*(4), 1584–1601.

Hay, C. (2006). Political Ontology. In R. E. Goodin and C. Tilly (Eds.), *The Oxford Handbook of Contextual Political Analysis* (pp. 78–96). Oxford University Press.

Hayes, M., & Hibbing, M. V. (2017). The Symbolic Benefits of Descriptive and Substantive Representation. *Political Behavior, 39*(1), 31–50.

Hooghe, L., & Marks, G. (2004). Does Identity or Economic Rationality Drive Public Opinion on European Integration? *PS: Political Science & Politics, 37*(3), 415–420.

House of Commons Library (2021). Women in Politics and Public Life. Briefing paper 01250, 2 March 2021. https://assets-learning.parliament.uk/uploads/2021/03/Teacher-Network-Briefing-Paper-Women-in-Politics-and-Public-Life-pdf.pdf.

Howarth, D. R., Norval, A. J., & Stavrakakis, Y. (2000). *Discourse Theory and Political Analysis: Identities, Hegemonies and Social Change.* Manchester University Press.

Inglehart, R., & Flanagan, S. C. (1987). Value Change in Industrial Societies. *American Political Science Review, 81*(4), 1289–1319.

Invernizzi-Accetti, C., & Wolkenstein, F. (2017). The Crisis of Party Democracy, Cognitive Mobilization, and the Case for Making Parties More Deliberative. *American Political Science Review, 111*(1), 97–109.

Iyengar, S., Lelkes, Y., Levendusky, M., Malhotra, N., & Westwood, S. J. (2019). The Origins and Consequences of Affective Polarization in the United States. *Annual Review of Political Science, 22*(1), 129–146.

Jacobs, L. R., & Shapiro, R. Y. (2000). *Politicians Don't Pander: Political Manipulation and the Loss of Democratic Responsiveness.* The University of Chicago Press.

Jäger, A., & Borriello, A. (2020). Left-Populism on Trial: Laclauian Politics in Theory and Practice. *Theory & Event, 23*(3), 740–764.

Kam, C. J. (2009). Party Discipline and Parliamentary Politics. Cambridge University Press.

Katz, R. S., & Mair, P. (2009). The Cartel Party Thesis: A Restatement. *Perspectives on Politics, 7*(4), 753–766.

Kellermann, M. (2015). Electoral Vulnerability, Constituency Focus, and Parliamentary Questions in the House of Commons. *British Journal of Politics and International Relations, 18*(1), 90–106.

Kelsen, H. (2013). *The Essence and Value of Democracy.* Rowman & Littlefield.

Kim, S.-H., Scheufele, D. A., & Shanahan, J. (2005). Who Cares about the Issues? Issue Voting and the Role of News Media during the 2000 U.S. Presidential Election. *Journal of Communication, 55*(1), 103–121.

Krook, M. L. (2010). *Quotas for Women in Politics: Gender and Candidate Selection Reform Worldwide*. Oxford University Press.

Krook, M. L., & O'Brien, D. Z. (2012). All the President's Men? The Appointment of Female Cabinet Ministers Worldwide. *The Journal of Politics, 74*(3), 840–855.

Laclau, E. (1990). *New Reflections on the Revolution of Our Time* (1. publ. ed.). Verso.

Laclau, E. (2005). *On Populist Reason*. Verso.

Laclau, E., & Mouffe, C. (1985). *Hegemony and Socialist Strategy: Towards a Radical Democratic Politics* (1. publ. ed.). Verso.

Lapinski, J., Levendusky, M., Winneg, K., & Jamieson, K. H. (2016). What Do Citizens Want from Their Member of Congress? *Political Research Quarterly, 69*(3), 535–545.

Lawless, J. L. (2015). Female Candidates and Legislators. *Annual Review of Political Science, 18*(1), 349–366.

Lax, J. R., & Phillips, J. H. (2011). The Democratic Deficit in the States. *American Journal of Political Science, 56*(1), 148–166.

Leeper, T. J., & Slothuus, R. (2014). Political Parties, Motivated Reasoning, and Public Opinion Formation. *Political Psychology, 35*(1), 129–156.

Lefort, C. (1988). *Democracy and Political Theory* (D. Macey, Trans.). Polity Press.

Lehrer, R., Stöckle, P., & Juhl, S. (2024). Assessing the Relative Influence of Party Unity on Vote Choice: Evidence from a Conjoint Experiment. *Political Science Research and Methods, 12*(1), 220–228.

Lupia, A. (1994). Shortcuts versus Encyclopedias: Information and Voting Behavior in California Insurance Reform Elections. *American Political Science Review, 88*(1), 63–76.

Lupia, A., & McCubbins, M. D. (1998). *The Democratic Dilemma: Can Citizens Learn What They Need to Know?* Cambridge University Press.

Mair, P. (2013). *Ruling the Void: The Hollowing-Out of Western Democracy*. Verso Books.

Mansbridge, J. (1999). Should Blacks Represent Blacks and Women Represent Women? A Contingent "Yes." *The Journal of Politics, 61*(3), 628–657.

Mansbridge, J. (2003). Rethinking Representation. *American Political Science Review, 97*(4), 515–528.

Mansbridge, J. (2005). Quota Problems: Combating the Dangers of Essentialism. *Politics & Gender, 1*(4), 622–638.

Mansbridge, J. (2009). A "Selection Model" of Political Representation. *Journal of Political Philosophy, 17*(4), 369–398.

Mansbridge, J. (2011). Clarifying the Concept of Representation. *American Political Science Review, 105*(3), 621–630.

Mansbridge, J. (2018). A Deliberative Theory of Interest Representation. In M. P. Petracca (Ed.), *The Politics of Interests* (pp. 32–57). Routledge.

Mattinson, D. (2019). All bets are off if Boris Johnson calls an early election. *The Guardian*. https://www.theguardian.com/politics/2019/jul/27/boris-johnson-early-election-dilemma.

Mayne, Q., & Hakhverdian, A. (2016). Ideological Congruence and Citizen Satisfaction: Evidence from 25 Advanced Democracies. *Comparative Political Studies, 50*(6), 822–849.

McKay, L. (2020). Does Constituency Focus Improve Attitudes to MPs? A Test for the UK. *Journal of Legislative Studies, 26*(1), 1–26.

Medina, J. (2023). *The Epistemology of Protest: Silencing, Epistemic Activism, and the Communicative Life of Resistance*. Oxford University Press.

Mendelberg, T., Karpowitz, C. F., & Goedert, N. (2014). Does Descriptive Representation Facilitate Women's Distinctive Voice? How Gender Composition and Decision Rules Affect Deliberation. *American Journal of Political Science, 58*(2), 291–306.

Miller, S. (2009). *The Moral Foundations of Social Institutions*. Cambridge University Press.

Miller, W. E., & Stokes, D. E. (1963). Constituency Influence in Congress. *American Political Science Review, 57*(1), 45–56.

Montanaro, L. (2018). Who Counts as a Democratic Representative? On Claims of Self-Appointed Representation. In D. Castiglione, & J. Pollak (Eds.), *Creating Political Presence: The New Politics of Democratic Representation* (pp. 195–212). University of Chicago Press.

Müller, W. C. (2003). Political Parties in Parliamentary Democracies: Making Delegation and Accountability Work. *European Journal of Political Research, 37*(3), 309–333.

Neblo, M. A., Esterling, K. M., Kennedy, R. P., Lazer, D. M. J., & Sokhey, A. E. (2010). Who Wants to Deliberate – and Why? *American Political Science Review, 104*(3), 566–583.

Neblo, M. A., Esterling, K. M., & Lazer, D. (2018). *Politics with the People: Building a Directly Representative Democracy*. Cambridge University Press.

Norris, P., & Lovenduski, J. (1995). *Political Recruitment: Gender, Race and Class in the British Parliament*. Cambridge University Press.

O'Brien, D. Z., & Piscopo, J. M. (2019). The Impact of Women in Parliament. In S. Franceschet, M. L. Krook, & N. Tan (Eds.), *The Palgrave Handbook of Women's Political Rights* (pp. 53–72). Palgrave Macmillan.

Papavero, L. C., & Zucchini, F. (2018). Gender and Party Cohesion in the Italian Parliament: A Spatial Analysis. *Italian Political Science Review/Rivista Italiana di Scienza Politica, 48*(2), 243–264.

Pearson, K., & Dancey, L. (2011). Speaking for the Underrepresented in the House of Representatives: Voicing Women's Interests in a Partisan Era. *Politics & Gender, 7*(4), 493–519.

Pennebaker, J. W., Boyd, R. L., Jordan, K., & Blackburn, K. (2015). *The Development and Psychometric Properties of LIWC2015*. University of Texas at Austin.

Pettit, P. (2010). Varieties of Public Representation. In I. Shapiro, S. C. Stokes, E. J. Wood, & A. S. Kirshner (Eds.), *Political Representation* (pp. 61–89). Cambridge University Press.

Pitkin, H. (1967). *The Concept of Representation*. University of California Press.

Powell, G. B. (2004). Political Representation in Comparative Politics. *Annual Review of Political Science, 7*(1), 273–296.

Prescott-Smith, S. (2019). *Which issues will decide the general election?* https://yougov.co.uk/topics/politics/articles-reports/2019/11/07/which-issues-will-decide-general-election.

Proctor, K. (2019). Labour Poised to Block Bid for 12 December General Election. *The Guardian*. https://www.theguardian.com/politics/2019/oct/24/labour-poised-to-block-offer-of-12-december-general-election.

Rehfeld, A. (2005). *The Concept of Constituency*. Cambridge University Press.

Rehfeld, A. (2009). Representation Rethought: On Trustees, Delegates, and Gyroscopes in the Study of Political Representation and Democracy. *American Political Science Review, 103*(2), 214–230.

Reingold, B. (2000). *Representing Women: Sex, Gender and Legislative Behavior in Arizona and California*. University of North Carolina Press.

Reingold, B. (2003). *Representing Women: Sex, Gender, and Legislative Behavior in Arizona and California*. University of North Carolina Press.

Rodriguez, P. L., & Spirling, A. (2022). Word Embeddings: What Works, What Doesn't, and How to Tell the Difference for Applied Research. *The Journal of Politics, 84*(1), 101–115.

Rosenbluth, F., & Shapiro, I. (2018). *Responsible Parties: Saving Democracy from Itself*. Yale University Press.

Rosset, J., Giger, N., & Bernauer, J. (2017). I the People? Self-Interest and Demand for Government Responsiveness. *Comparative Political Studies, 50*(6), 794–821.

Sabl, A. (2015). The Two Cultures of Democratic Theory: Responsiveness, Democratic Quality, and the Empirical-Normative Divide. *Perspectives on Politics, 13*(2), 345–365.

Saward, M. (2009). Authorisation and Authenticity: Representation and the Unelected*. *Journal of Political Philosophy*, *17*(1), 1–22.

Saward, M. (2010). *The Representative Claim*. Oxford University Press.

Saward, M. (2014). Shape-Shifting Representation. *American Political Science Review*, *108*(4), 723–736.

Saward, M. (2018). Liminal Representation. In D. Castiglione, & J. Pollak (Eds.), *Creating Political Presence: The New Politics of Democratic Representation* (pp. 285–306). University of Chicago Press.

Saward, M. (2019). Theorizing about Democracy. *Democratic Theory*, *6*(2), 1–11.

Schakel, W., & Van Der Pas, D. (2021). Degrees of Influence: Educational Inequality in Policy Representation. *European Journal of Political Research*, *60*(2), 418–437.

Schattschneider, E. E. (1942). *Party Government*. Transaction.

Schildkraut, D. J. (2013). The Complicated Constituency: A Study of Immigrant Opinions about Political Representation. *Politics, Groups and Identities*, *1*(1), 26–47.

Schwindt-Bayer, L. A. (2009). Making Quotas Work: The Effect of Gender Quota Laws On the Election of Women. *Legislative Studies Quarterly*, *34*(1), 5–28.

Searle, J. R. (1969). *Speech Acts: An Essay in the Philosophy of Language* (Vol. 626). Cambridge University Press.

Slapin, J. B., Kirkland, J. H., Lazzaro, J. A., Leslie, P. A., & O'Grady, T. (2018). Ideology, Grandstanding, and Strategic Party Disloyalty in the British Parliament. *American Political Science Review*, *112*(1), 15–30.

Sobolewska, M., McKee, R., & Campbell, R. (2018). Explaining Motivation to Represent: How Does Descriptive Representation Lead to Substantive Representation of Racial and Ethnic Minorities? *West European Politics*, *41*(6), 1237–1261.

Soroka, S. N., & Wlezien, C. (2010). *Degrees of Democracy: Politics, Public Opinion, and Policy*. Cambridge University Press.

Stimson, J. A. (1999). *Public Opinion in America: Moods, Cycles, and Swings*. Routledge.

Stimson, J. A., MacKuen, M. B., & Erikson, R. S. (1995). Dynamic Representation. *American Political Science Review*, *89*(3), 543–565.

Strøm, K., Müller, W. C., Bergman, T., & Nyblade, B. (2003). Dimensions of Citizen Control. In K. Strøm, W. C. Müller, & T. Bergman (Eds.), *Delegation and Accountability in Parliamentary Democracies* (pp. 651–706). Oxford University Press.

Teele, D. L., Kalla, J., & Rosenbluth, F. (2018). The Ties That Double Bind: Social Roles and Women's Underrepresentation in Politics. *American Political Science Review, 112*(3), 525–541.

Thomassen, J., & van Ham, C. (2014). Failing Political Representation or a Change in Kind? Models of Representation and Empirical Trends in Europe. *West European Politics, 37*(2), 400–419.

Thomassen, L. (2019). Representing the People: Laclau as a Theorist of Representation. *New Political Science, 41*(2), 329–344.

Thomsen, D. M., & King, A. S. (2020). Women's Representation and the Gendered Pipeline to Power. *American Political Science Review, 114*(4), 989–1000.

Truex, R. (2016). *Making Autocracy Work: Representation and Responsiveness in Modern China.* Cambridge University Press.

Urbinati, N. (2011). Representative Democracy and Its Critics. In S. Alonso, J. Keane, & W. Merkel (Eds.), *The Future of Representative Democracy* (pp. 23–49). Cambridge University Press.

Urbinati, N. (2019). Representative Constructivism's Conundrum. In L. Disch, M. van de Sande, & N. Urbinati (Eds.), *The Constructivist Turn in Political Representation* (pp. 182–201). Edinburgh University Press.

Van Biezen, I. (2012). Constitutionalizing Party Democracy: The Constitutive Codification of Political Parties in Post-War Europe. *British Journal of Political Science, 42*(1), 187–212.

Van Evera, S. (2016). *Guide to Methods for Students of Political Science.* Cornell University Press.

van Ham, C., Thomassen, J. J., Aarts, K., & Andeweg, R. B. (2017). *Myth and Reality of the Legitimacy Crisis: Explaining Trends and Cross-National Differences in Established Democracies.* Oxford University Press.

Walsh, K. C. (2002). Enlarging Representation: Women Bringing Marginalized Perspectives to Floor Debate in the House of Representatives. In C. S. Rosenthal (Ed.), *Women Transforming Congress* (pp. 370–396). University of Oklahoma Press.

Wängnerud, L. (2009). Women in Parliaments: Descriptive and Substantive Representation. *Annual Review of Political Science, 12*, 51–69.

Ward, D., Kim, J. H., Graham, M., & Tavits, M. (2015). How Economic Integration Affects Party Issue Emphases. *Comparative Political Studies, 48*(10), 1227–1259.

Warren, M. E. (2017). A Problem-Based Approach to Democratic Theory. *American Political Science Review, 111*(1), 39–53.

Weber, M. (1978). *Economy and Society: An Outline of Interpretive Sociology.* University of California Press.

Weber, M. (2013). *Economy and Society* (Vol. 1). University of California Press.

Westphal, M. (2019). Overcoming the Institutional Deficit of Agonistic Democracy. *Res Publica*, *25*(2), 187–210.

White, J., & Ypi, L. (2016). *The Meaning of Partisanship*. Oxford University Press.

Wojcik, S., & Mullenax, S. (2017). Men Idle, Women Network: How Networks Help Female Legislators Succeed. *Legislative Studies Quarterly*, *42*(4), 579–610.

Wolak, J. (2017). Public Expectations of State Legislators. *Legislative Studies Quarterly*, *42*(2), 175–209.

Wolkenstein, F., & Wratil, C. (2021). Multidimensional Representation. *American Journal of Political Science*, *65*(4), 862–876.

Wratil, C., & Wäckerle, J. (2023). Majority Representation and Public Legitimacy: Survey-Experimental Evidence from the European Union. *European Journal of Political Research*, *62*(1), 285–307.

Zollinger, D. (2024). Cleavage Identities in Voters' Own Words: Harnessing Open-Ended Survey Responses. *American Journal of Political Science*, *68*(1), 139–159.

Acknowledgments

We are indebted to Anna-Maria Rebel, Lorka Ó hAnnracháin and Laura Pfisterer for their assistance on this project as well as to Jack Blumenau and Ben Lauderdale, who respectively shared the UK House of Commons speech and divisions data with us. Fabio Wolkenstein would like to acknowledge financial support by the University of Aarhus. Previous versions of Section 4 were presented at the EPSA General Conference 2021, the ECPR General Conference 2022, and the University of Basel in 2022. We are grateful for excellent comments and suggestions by two anonymous referees and Stuart Soroka as series editor.

Cambridge Elements

Politics and Communication

Stuart Soroka
University of California

Stuart Soroka is a Professor in the Department of Communication at the University of California, Los Angeles, and Adjunct Research Professor at the Center for Political Studies at the Institute for Social Research, University of Michigan. His research focuses on political communication, political psychology, and the relationships between public policy, public opinion, and mass media. His books with Cambridge University Press include The Increasing Viability of Good News (2021, with Yanna Krupnikov), Negativity in Democratic Politics (2014), Information and Democracy (forthcoming, with Christopher Wlezien) and Degrees of Democracy (2010, with Christopher Wlezien).

About the Series

Cambridge Elements in Politics and Communication publishes research focused on the intersection of media, technology, and politics. The series emphasizes forward-looking reviews of the field, path-breaking theoretical and methodological innovations, and the timely application of social-scientific theory and methods to current developments in politics and communication around the world.

Cambridge Elements ≡

Politics and Communication

Elements in the Series

A full series listing is available at: www.cambridge.org/EPCM

Printed in the United States
by Baker & Taylor Publisher Services